STERLING BIOGRAPHIES

BABE RUTH

Legendary Slugger

David Fischer

STERLING

New York / London
www.sterlingpublishing.com/kids

To my loving family; providing a comfort the Babe never knew.

David Fischer
New Jersey, 2009

STERLING and the distinctive Sterling logo are registered trademarks of
Sterling Publishing Co., Inc.

Library of Congress Cataloging-in-Publication Data
Fischer, David, 1963–
  Babe Ruth : legendary slugger / by David Fischer.
     p. cm. — (Sterling biographies)
  Includes bibliographical references and index.
  ISBN 978-1-4027-7147-7 (hardcover) — ISBN 978-1-4027-6366-3 (pbk.)
  1. Ruth, Babe, 1895–1948—Juvenile literature. 2. Baseball players—United States—
Biography—Juvenile literature. I. Title.
  GV865.R8F57 2010
  796.357092—dc22
  [B]
                                                 2009024214
Lot #: 10 9 8 7 6 5 4 3 2 1
12/09

Published by Sterling Publishing Co., Inc.
387 Park Avenue South, New York, NY 10016
© 2010 by David Fischer

Distributed in Canada by Sterling Publishing
c/o Canadian Manda Group, 165 Dufferin Street
Toronto, Ontario, Canada M6K 3H6
Distributed in the United Kingdom by GMC Distribution Services
Castle Place, 166 High Street, Lewes, East Sussex, England BN7 1XU
Distributed in Australia by Capricorn Link (Australia) Pty. Ltd.
P.O. Box 704, Windsor, NSW 2756, Australia

Printed in China
All rights reserved

Sterling ISBN 978-1-4027-7147-7 (hardcover)
      ISBN 978-1-4027-6366-3 (paperback)

Image research by Jim Gigliotti and James Buckley, Jr.

For information about custom editions, special sales, premium and corporate
purchases, please contact Sterling Special Sales Department at 800-805-5489
or specialsales@sterlingpublishing.com.

Contents

INTRODUCTION: Larger-than-Life Hero............... 1

CHAPTER 1: Saloonkeeper's Son 2

CHAPTER 2: A Fresh Start 10

CHAPTER 3: Finding Direction...................... 18

CHAPTER 4: Becoming the Babe..................... 28

CHAPTER 5: From Baltimore to Boston 36

CHAPTER 6: Pitching for a Living 44

CHAPTER 7: The Changing World 54

CHAPTER 8: Babe's Big Move 65

CHAPTER 9: Guts and Glory 76

CHAPTER 10: A Living Legend...................... 88

CHAPTER 11: The End of an Era 96

CHAPTER 12: Heading for Home 104

GLOSSARY 116

BIBLIOGRAPHY.................................. 117

SOURCE NOTES 118

IMAGE CREDITS 122

ABOUT THE AUTHOR............................ 122

INDEX... 123

Events in the Life of Babe Ruth

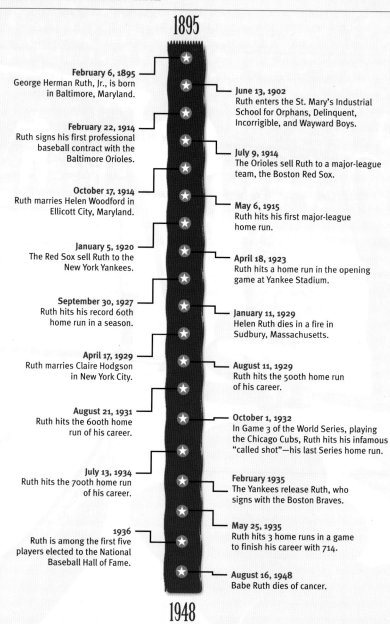

1895

February 6, 1895
George Herman Ruth, Jr., is born in Baltimore, Maryland.

June 13, 1902
Ruth enters the St. Mary's Industrial School for Orphans, Delinquent, Incorrigible, and Wayward Boys.

February 22, 1914
Ruth signs his first professional baseball contract with the Baltimore Orioles.

July 9, 1914
The Orioles sell Ruth to a major-league team, the Boston Red Sox.

October 17, 1914
Ruth marries Helen Woodford in Ellicott City, Maryland.

May 6, 1915
Ruth hits his first major-league home run.

January 5, 1920
The Red Sox sell Ruth to the New York Yankees.

April 18, 1923
Ruth hits a home run in the opening game at Yankee Stadium.

September 30, 1927
Ruth hits his record 60th home run in a season.

January 11, 1929
Helen Ruth dies in a fire in Sudbury, Massachusetts.

April 17, 1929
Ruth marries Claire Hodgson in New York City.

August 11, 1929
Ruth hits the 500th home run of his career.

August 21, 1931
Ruth hits the 600th home run of his career.

October 1, 1932
In Game 3 of the World Series, playing the Chicago Cubs, Ruth hits his infamous "called shot"—his last Series home run.

July 13, 1934
Ruth hits the 700th home run of his career.

February 1935
The Yankees release Ruth, who signs with the Boston Braves.

1936
Ruth is among the first five players elected to the National Baseball Hall of Fame.

May 25, 1935
Ruth hits 3 home runs in a game to finish his career with 714.

August 16, 1948
Babe Ruth dies of cancer.

1948

Larger-than-Life Hero

Where the Babe was, center stage was.

—*Legendary sportswriter Roger Kahn*

The New York Yankees were playing the Chicago Cubs in Game Three of the 1932 **World Series**. The score was tied 4–4 in the fifth inning with Babe Ruth coming to bat. The players on the Cubs' bench yelled at the Yankee **slugger**, teasing and insulting him. Ruth took two strikes from pitcher Charlie Root and then stepped out of the batter's box.

That's all true. No question. What happened next, however, remains a legend to this day.

Some folks claim Ruth held up one finger, indicating that he needed only one more pitch to score. Others claim he held up two fingers, indicating that Root had thrown only two strikes—Ruth wasn't out yet. Still others say he pointed to the heckling Cubs. But many observers insist that Ruth pointed straight out to the center-field bleachers. Was he saying he was about to hit a **home run**?

Whatever he did, Ruth waited for Root's next pitch, took a mighty swing, and launched a homer deep into the center-field bleachers—right where he had apparently pointed. Had Ruth really been so bold as to predict his home run? Ruth himself never really said one way or another. But making legends and leaving people awestruck was what Babe Ruth was all about.

CHAPTER 1

Saloonkeeper's Son

I was a bum when I was a kid.

Georn Herman Ruth, Jr., was born in Baltimore, Maryland, on February 6, 1895 (though his parents mistakenly told him it had been 1894). As he was growing up, he was called Little George; his father was Big George. He would not become "Babe" Ruth until he started playing professional baseball. Little George was the oldest of eight children born to George and Kate Schaumberger Ruth. Kate Ruth was a small woman, standing four feet ten inches tall, and she was nineteen years old when Little George was born. She gave birth to seven other children—three more boys and four girls—but only one other child,

a daughter, survived past childhood. Little George was five years old when his sister Mary Margaret was born. He called her Mamie.

The young George Ruth had a mop of

This photo of Babe Ruth—who was known as George Herman Ruth, Jr., at the time—was taken in 1898, when he was three years old.

thick, dark brown hair. With his round face and wide nose, he would grow up to look just like his father. Big George bounced around from one job to another. He worked at a grocery store and then as a lightning rod salesman, with no success, before trying his luck as a saloonkeeper. George's father kept the saloon open day and night, often working sixteen-hour shifts. Two years before Ruth's birth, a terrible economic crisis had hit the United States. This time in our history is known as the Panic of 1893. Trying to keep the family business afloat left Big George little time or energy to help care for his two children.

Kate Ruth is a bit of a mystery. Not much is known about her, but apparently she suffered from depression, a serious mental illness. Little George was not mature enough to understand his father's financial problems or his mother's poor mental health, and Mamie was too young to offer her older brother any emotional support. Little George felt unwanted, abandoned, and alone. "I hardly knew my parents," said Ruth, "and I think my mother hated me."

Pigtown

Like most of their Baltimore neighbors, the Ruths were a poor family struggling to make ends meet. Times were tough, and money was scarce. During Ruth's early years, the family moved from one rundown apartment to another in a rough-and-tumble Baltimore neighborhood near the waterfront.

By the turn of the century, the four Ruths had settled into a cramped, three-room apartment above the saloon that Big George opened at 406 Conway Street. The barroom was called Ruth's Café. It was located on the spot that is now center field at Oriole Park at Camden Yards, home to Baltimore's **major-league** baseball team, the Orioles.

Financial Hardships

The Panic of 1893 was caused by a drain on the U.S. Treasury's gold reserves, which resulted in the failure of more than five hundred banks. Across the country, more than fifteen thousand businesses closed. Two of every ten workers had no jobs. The stock market took a massive nosedive. It would not be until 1897, as young George Ruth was growing up, that recovery began. The Ruth family, like millions of others, struggled to earn money to buy the things they needed. The Ruths always found a place to live, but many others were not as lucky. The Panic of 1893 was the most severe economic crisis in our nation's history to that point.

Financial troubles in 1893 set off a wave of panic in the stock markets, which is depicted in this drawing from that year.

Oriole Park at Camden Yards is the current home of the American League's Baltimore Orioles. The saloon that Babe Ruth's father owned was in an area now covered by center field at the stadium.

The area where Ruth grew up was called Pigtown. The district got its name from the herds of pigs that ran through the neighborhood alleys on their way from the stockyard to the slaughterhouse. People living there are said to have grabbed pigs off the streets to feed their family. The sound of squealing pigs was ever present.

When George reached the age of six, Mr. and Mrs. Ruth enrolled their son in school. Little George quickly discovered that he could not abide by the rules and regulations he was forced to follow. Every day he pretended to go to school, and every day he'd sneak away. **Truancy** became his daily routine. "The truant officer spent more time at our house than his own," his sister said years later. "I don't know how Babe did it. I'd even see him close the school door behind him. But somehow he always got out."

After escaping from the schoolyard, George wandered the gritty streets of Baltimore with other aimless, delinquent boys. These mischief makers were a poor influence on George, who always took a dare. He engaged in such disruptive behavior as breaking windows, stealing fruit, and throwing eggs at people. "I was a bum when I was a kid," Ruth admitted.

"Rotten Start"

The early years of Babe Ruth's life were times of self-reliance. The neighborhood storeowners thought that he was an orphan, because he spent so much time running in the streets in dirty clothes and because the little food he ate was usually stolen. He had no strong family life to give him support. For the most part, Little George was left alone like a stray cat to fend for himself. "I had a rotten start," he said years later, "and it took me a long time to get my bearings."

Little George was big for his age, and he was growing up fast—too fast. During the day, George's parents rarely knew where he was. Many an evening he spent washing dishes in the family saloon. A barroom is a bad place for a boy who is already heading in the wrong direction. By the time he was seven years old, George was drinking the alcohol left at the bottom of other people's glasses. He also developed the nasty habit of chewing tobacco. "Not that I enjoyed it," he remembered, "but from my observations around the saloon, it seemed the normal thing to do."

For the most part, Little George was left alone like a stray cat to fend for himself.

Babe (second from right) was a teenager when this photo was taken in Ruth's Café in 1916 or 1917. Babe's father, Big George, is at the far right.

One of young Ruth's favorite pranks was stealing from his father's cash drawer and using the money to buy ice cream for the neighborhood kids. "Looking back on my early boyhood, I honestly don't remember being aware of the difference between right and wrong," he said. "If my parents had something that I wanted very badly, I took it."

Tipping Point

By 1902, George had become such a difficult and uncontrollable child that his parents gave up their legal right to care for their only son. How this came to be is debated. Some accounts describe a fight that broke out in the saloon one day. The brawl turned violent, and a gun was fired. When police arrived on the scene, officers learned that Little George was in the barroom at the time of the shooting. Then they discovered that he never went to school. Back then, the city of Baltimore rounded up the worst of the young troublemakers and carted them off to a reform school for rehabilitation.

A court of law may have ordered the Ruths to place their son in such an institution for his own well-being. Or the Ruths may have realized on their own that their son would be better off in more stable surroundings. Whichever the case, Little George's life was about to make a radical change. In the spring of 1902, George and Kate Ruth filed court papers to classify their son as beyond their control. Little George's legal custody was now officially transferred to the brothers of the order of St. Francis

This photo is of a marketplace in Baltimore in the 1900s. Babe Ruth, who was born in 1895, was a child at the time.

Xavier. The brothers were not priests, but they did take vows of modesty, chastity, and obedience.

The brothers operated the St. Mary's Industrial School for Boys. Helping disadvantaged youth is one of the Xaverian Brothers' main missions. The Baltimore school was opened in 1866 to care for the growing number of young boys who were left orphans in the aftermath of the Civil War. As years went by, the school accepted a wider range of needy children. By the turn of the century, the school's official name was St. Mary's Industrial School for Orphans, Delinquent, Incorrigible (meaning disobedient), and Wayward Boys. "I was listed as an incorrigible," said Ruth, "and I guess I was."

On June 13, 1902, Mr. Ruth hoisted his teary-eyed, seven-year-old son aboard the Wilkens Avenue trolley for a ride across town. They got off at a stop four miles southwest of Pigtown. There, Little George saw St. Mary's, sprawled on several acres atop a hillside, for the first time. He was scared. Swearing to forevermore be a respectable boy, he begged his father to please take him home. But it was too late for apologies. George Herman Ruth, Jr., would spend most of the next twelve years inside the walls of St. Mary's as a ward of the Xaverian Brothers.

CHAPTER 2

A Fresh Start

[Brother Matthias] taught me to read and write—and he taught me the difference between right and wrong.

The St. Mary's campus consisted of six gray stone buildings between three and five stories high. More than eight hundred boys ages seven to twenty-one lived at the school. The boys slept in four dormitories, each with about two hundred cots. Besides shelter, St. Mary's provided the boys with three meals a day, clean clothing, an education, job training, and much-needed discipline.

Some boys, like George, were sent to St. Mary's because their families had neglected them. Some were orphans in need of a place to live. (This is how the myth of Ruth being an orphan came to be.) Still others were runaways, truants, and boys who had been in trouble with the police. Thirty Xaverian Brothers took care of

Besides shelter, St. Mary's provided the boys with three meals a day, clean clothing, an education, job training, and much-needed discipline.

approximately eight hundred boys at St. Mary's. The brothers acted as parents, teachers, coaches, and cooks. The boys now had people who cared for them—and cared about them.

Trade School

Xaverian Brothers are men who vow to lead a devout and religious life. They follow Catholic guidelines, but the school took in boys of all faiths. The brothers believed that their main objective was to turn out respectable young men who were prepared for life as adults. Education was emphasized. Students attended morning and afternoon classes until their thirteenth birthday. Teenagers had only morning classes, and spent their afternoons learning a trade. The brothers taught them the skills to be carpenters, electricians, painters, tailors, typesetters, shoemakers, launderers, gardeners, farmers, and bakers. The brothers were willing to teach any boy who was willing to learn.

George worked as a carpenter for a time and then took up shirt making. Working in the tailor shop, he had a job putting

In this photo, students in a trade school in the early 1900s (this one was in New York) learn about plumbing. Babe Ruth learned various trades at his school in Baltimore.

collars and cuffs on shirts. Later, he began sewing shirts for the boys at school to wear. He was paid six cents for each shirt he made. At his best, he claimed he could sew a shirt in fifteen minutes. He used the money he earned sewing shirts to buy candy at the canteen, which he shared freely with smaller kids.

From the brothers, George Ruth learned the values of hard work, honesty, and integrity and the importance of learning a trade. Their influence would have a profound impact on the wild youngster. In later years, the Babe was not shy about expressing fondness for his old school. "I'm proud of St. Mary's," he would often say; to prove it, "I will be happy to bop anybody on the beezer [nose] who speaks ill of it."

Big Brother

The boys were expected to stay at St. Mary's until they turned twenty-one, and most did. Although the grounds were surrounded by high brick walls, wooden fences, and stout iron gates—and the boys there called themselves inmates—the school was not a prison. No security guards prevented a boy from running away, yet few ever tried. Those who did had to face Brother Matthias, the school disciplinarian and a hulk of a man.

No security guards prevented a boy from running away, yet few ever tried.

Standing six feet six inches tall and weighing as much as three hundred pounds, Brother Matthias was a commanding physical presence. Wearing the long, black robe that was the brothers' standard uniform, Matthias looked like an enormous grizzly bear. In fact, he was so large that the door to his room opened outward rather than inward to accommodate an oversize bed.

This is Brother Matthias from the St. Mary's Industrial School. Brother Matthias had a profound and lasting impact on Babe Ruth's life.

To George, the brother was more than an authority figure. When he came to St. Mary's, George could not read or write. To catch up on his learning, he had to attend classes with younger children. Older boys teased him about this, and their laughter made him feel awkward and embarrassed. Working with Brother Matthias, George would eventually learn reading and writing.

"It was at St. Mary's that I met and learned to love the greatest man I've ever known," said Ruth. "His name was Brother Matthias. . . . He taught me to read and write—and he taught me the difference between right and wrong."

The Boss

Brother Matthias was a strict, but reasonable, man. The children called him the Boss. They were in awe of this quiet giant, and he inspired their respect. "He was calm [and] considerate, and gave everyone a fair break," said a student. "But, brother, if you ever crossed him you were sure in trouble."

One afternoon, some students started roughhousing in the yard. Brother Matthias was called in. He broke up the fight without saying a word. He simply stood on a perch of high ground in the yard and looked out over the crowd of unruly students.

"A great silence came over the yard," Ruth recalled, "and the trouble stopped immediately. He was that kind of fellow. It wasn't that we were afraid of Brother Matthias. Some men just have an ability to command respect, and love, and Brother Matthias was one of these."

Staying for Good

To the brothers, all the boys were the same—they were boys whose families could not take care of them—and all boys were treated equally. Boys who disobeyed were punished with a spanking by leather strap. Spankings were meant to be hurtful, for the brothers relied on discipline to restore and maintain order at the school.

George Ruth was an "inmate" at St. Mary's for nearly twelve years. In 1912, when George was seventeen years old, Kate Ruth died, at age thirty-nine from tuberculosis. While George was at St. Mary's, no relative or friend ever came to visit him. "I guess I'm too ugly," Ruth joked when a classmate asked why he never had a visitor.

George developed sympathy for children who had been abandoned by their

"I guess I'm too ugly," Ruth joked when a classmate asked why he never had a visitor.

families. This empathy stayed with him throughout adulthood, and even when he became a famous baseball player, he would still visit orphanages as often as he could. Ruth's compassion for children was well known. He often visited them in hospitals, promising to hit home runs for them, and then followed through on his word.

Hateful Name

George Ruth was not transformed into a prince at St. Mary's overnight. He still played practical jokes. He still sometimes wandered off on his own to smoke a cigarette. And he never backed down from a fight.

By the time he was twelve, he had a reputation as an overactive child. As one of the brothers remembered, "He was livelier than most of the boys, full of mischief. There was nothing timid about him. He was an aggressive, shouting boy who was always wrestling around with the others. He held his own, too."

The fighting stemmed from a nickname that George hated. Nearly all the boys at school had a nickname; often it was a comment on an obvious physical characteristic. Nicknames such as Skinny, Kid, Lefty, and Red were common.

As soon as Ruth arrived at St. Mary's, he was called a **racial slur**. The nickname mocked his full lips, which resembled those of the day's African American **stereotype**. The nickname was particularly hurtful because at the time, African Americans were not treated as citizens with equal rights. As a boy at St. Mary's, George was often subjected to the same **bigotry** and second-class treatment that black U.S. citizens received. One biographer wrote that Ruth "had facial characteristics—the lips, the nose—that gave him a mixed-race look in a time and environment when a mixed-race look was not a good thing to have."

This situation offended Ruth. Knowing only one way to defend himself, George fought back by clobbering anyone who

National Shame

The United States was not always friendly to people of color. For decades, black U.S. citizens did not enjoy the same rights and privileges as white citizens. Even though the Fourteenth Amendment, adopted in 1868, guaranteed equal treatment to blacks, many social inequalities still existed. Black Americans did not have the same job opportunities as whites, and they were often the victims of small-minded **racists**.

Racial **discrimination** was a serious social problem throughout the nation. Throughout the South, blacks and whites were kept separate in schools and in restaurants. Black Americans were forced to sit in the backs of public buses, in separate sections of baseball stadiums, and in the balconies of movie theaters. They even had to drink from different water fountains and sleep in separate hotels.

When Babe Ruth played, Major League Baseball in the United States was restricted to whites only. At the time, black players participated in the Negro Leagues during the summer, and during the winter they played in the Puerto Rican League. Not until Ruth had been retired from Major League Baseball for twelve years could a dark-skinned athlete dream of playing before sold-out crowds in Boston's Fenway Park or New York's Yankee Stadium. What made the dream possible was that on April 15, 1947, a black American named Jackie Robinson made history by playing in the major leagues as a member of the Brooklyn Dodgers.

This undated photograph shows separate drinking fountains for white Americans and African Americans.

Babe Ruth (top row, far left) was a member of the St. Mary's baseball squad when he posed with his teammates for this photo in the early 1910s.

dared call him that nickname to his face. Brother Matthias urged George to channel his anger into baseball. This was a turning point in his life. George spent all his free time on the baseball field, honing his athletic skills and thriving under the tutelage of Brother Matthias. Still, the hateful nickname was one that in his childhood Ruth heard a hundred times a day. Two decades later, as Ruth was rewriting the baseball record book, rival players would also accuse him of having African American relatives, a claim that has never been proven.

CHAPTER 3

Finding Direction

I never would have played [baseball] professionally if Brother Matthias hadn't . . . changed not only my position on the field but the course of my life.

St. Mary's offered many sports—baseball, football, volleyball, soccer, swimming, boxing, wrestling, and basketball—but baseball was the favorite. The school had more than forty baseball teams, and the brothers organized tournaments between different dormitories for all age groups.

Games were played on two dusty ball fields in a large, open space between the dormitories. The fields were called the Big Yard and the Little Yard. Boys fifteen and older played on the Big Yard; younger children played on the Little Yard. Most teams from the school played one another. The elite teams also played against teams from other schools. The brothers coached them all.

George Ruth played baseball the first day he arrived at St. Mary's. Brother Matthias was choosing sides for a game when he noticed the new boy at the edge of the field. He called for George to join in. Brother Matthias tossed him a right-handed catcher's mitt, not knowing George was a natural left-hander. George put the glove designed for the left hand on his right hand (the wrong hand) and started to play. Despite this disadvantage, the

Baseball gloves looked different in the early twentieth century than they do now. This is one of Babe Ruth's gloves in the collection of the National Baseball Hall of Fame and Museum in Cooperstown, New York.

gangly kid who walked with his toes pointing inward possessed a natural talent for playing baseball.

It was very clear to Brother Matthias that George had been blessed with superior hand-eye coordination, extraordinary reflexes, and remarkable athleticism. In the hopes that George would concentrate on developing his special gift, Brother Matthias offered to be the boy's personal coach. Brother Matthias thought the game would be a way to teach George discipline. He also hoped that George's baseball talent would be a way for him to win the admiration of the other boys.

Coming of Age

George learned the game of baseball from Brother Matthias during their long practice sessions on the Big Yard. They practiced together throughout the year, even when it was not baseball season. Brother Matthias drilled George by the hour, correcting any mistakes he made. "It wasn't that I was his 'pet,'" said Ruth. "But he concentrated on me. He studied what few gifts I had and drew these out of me and amplified them. He always built me [up]."

As George entered his teenage years, he stood close to six feet tall and weighed 160 pounds. His extraordinary power hitting won many games for St. Mary's and brought him the respect of other boys. He still had classes with younger children, but the baseball field was a different story. There, he played with the oldest players at the school, and he was better than any of them.

Because of his size and his athletic gifts, George was playing baseball with boys several years older. He was nine when he played with the twelve-year-olds, and twelve when he played with the sixteen-year-olds. By the time he was sixteen, he was already a member of the elite traveling team playing alongside and against men as old as twenty-one. During baseball season at St. Mary's, George played more than two hundred games—more games than a professional baseball player would play. Ruth was the star catcher on a team called the Red Sox. All of St. Mary's

Babe Ruth (right) was a catcher for St. Mary's when this 1912 photo was taken. He played that position until his coaches realized he could be an overpowering pitcher.

teams were named after major-league teams. In 1912, Ruth's team won the school championship.

Natural Talent

It was as a member of the St. Mary's Red Sox that Ruth first took the mound as a pitcher. The starting pitcher was being walloped by the batters on the opposing team. George began laughing and jeering him. Hearing George's taunts, Brother Matthias decided to give George a lesson in humility. The brother stopped the game and told Ruth, "If you know so much about pitching, why not do it yourself?" Ruth did not know how to pitch, but he didn't back down from the challenge. He walked to the mound and surprised everyone by throwing the ball harder than any of the other kids. A great pitcher was born.

"As I took the position, I felt a strange relationship with that pitcher's mound," he said. "I felt, somehow, as if I had been born out there and that this was a kind of home for me. Pitching just felt like the most natural thing in the world. Striking out batters was easy."

With Brother Matthias's coaching, Ruth switched positions from catcher to pitcher. Brother Matthias taught Ruth the art of pitching: how to control the ball and how to deceive the batter by varying the speed of his pitches.

Brother Matthias taught Ruth the art of pitching: how to control the ball and how to deceive the batter by varying the speed of his pitches.

"I never would have played [baseball] professionally if Brother Matthias hadn't put me in my place one day and changed not only my position on the field but the course of my life," he said.

Schoolboy Star

By the spring of 1912, when he was seventeen years old, George was a sturdy 185 pounds. He could run, throw, field, and hit with power. George was something special on a baseball field. Whenever he'd come to bat, the opposing outfielders moved from their normal position on the Big Yard to near the infield on the Little Yard, nearly three hundred feet away. The boys playing on the Little Yard, knowing who was taking his turn at bat, stopped their own game to watch George's swings. He often smashed a ball onto the Little Yard.

George's baseball feats began to attract attention among the entire school. In 1912, the *St. Mary's Saturday Evening Star*, the school newspaper, mentioned his name for the first time, reporting on a game in which the seventeen-year-old Ruth struck out six batters while pitching. He also hit a ball out of the playing yard for a home run. Time and again, George's pitching success earned notice, and he also continued his outstanding hitting. By his own count, George hit 60 home runs in 1912 for the St. Mary's Red Sox.

Baseball became an obsession for him. He was all-consumed by it, and the more he played the game, the better he developed his skills.

Baseball was making an impact on Ruth's life. On the field, he was a success, and he was popular among his teammates. Other boys had once made fun of his looks, or had laughed at the way he walked with his toes pointing inward. Now those same boys accepted Ruth, and he was admired by his peers. Baseball became an obsession for him. He was all-consumed by it, and the more he played the game, the better he developed his skills.

Attracting Notice

When Ruth got too good to play at St. Mary's in the summer, Brother Matthias gave him permission to go outside the school on weekends to play in the local **amateur** leagues. Evidence from this time is a bit sketchy, but historians believe Ruth's name first appeared in the sports pages of a community newspaper on June 8, 1913. A week later, the *Baltimore American* described a left-handed schoolboy pitching star for the St. Patrick's Catholic Club named George "Roth" who struck out 12 batters in one game and 14 in another. Local Baltimore newspapers were soon touting George as "Roth the Speed Boy," in reference to his darting fastball pitch.

Before long, everyone would know George's name. On August 3, Ruth—now spelled properly—appeared in the lineup with another top-notch amateur team, the Bayonnes. He caught both games of a doubleheader and collected 3 hits. The newspaper billed him as "the Bayonne Fence Buster." In the future, George would have no shortage of colorful baseball-related nicknames.

George Ruth was beginning to earn a reputation as one of the best amateur players in Baltimore, and he was a symbol of school pride. By 1913, the eighteen-year-old Ruth was the star of the St. Mary's team and was recognized as the finest pitcher and batter the school had ever seen.

Feeling the Heat

The Xaverian Brothers also ran a boys' college, Mount St. Joseph's, in Baltimore, not far from St. Mary's. The college also had a baseball team, and the brothers argued in good-natured competition about which team was best. In the spring of 1913, Brother Gilbert, who coached the St. Joseph's team, began to

The Xaverian Brothers, some of whom are shown above playing croquet, also ran Mount St. Joseph's, a Baltimore college.

boast that he had a star pitcher of his own, Bill Morrisette. In response, the brothers at St. Mary's bragged that Ruth was the more talented pitcher.

To settle the score, the two schools decided to play a game. Excitement about the big game began to build for the boys of St. Mary's. They viewed St. Joseph's as a rich school down the road filled with snobby college boys, and they wanted desperately to win. Everyone was looking forward to the event of the season, when the dirt-poor, delinquent boys from the reformatory would play head-to-head against the well-to-do college kids.

About ten days before the game, so the story goes, George was nowhere to be found. The best player at St. Mary's was missing. The news sent the school into a panic. The brothers searched for George. It was determined that he had run away from school. The boys were stunned. Rumors spread about Ruth's disappearance. He had been gone for two days. The police were called in to search the Baltimore waterfront.

Eventually, Ruth was found hanging out near the pier and taken back to St. Mary's. He said he had returned voluntarily, but the other boys weren't buying that line. The pressure to play well in the big game had frightened him away.

After punishment for desertion, Brother Matthias explained to George how the boys of St. Mary's were counting on him to beat St. Joseph's. A remorseful Ruth didn't want to let down his teammates and friends. For the days leading up to the game, he worked diligently to loosen up his left arm (his throwing arm). He was a model of focus and determination, for he knew this would be his toughest test yet as a pitcher.

Impressing Mr. Dunn

On the morning of the big day, there was a festive atmosphere on campus. The grass and dirt infield was perfectly manicured. The outfield fences were covered with colorful banners. A noisy crowd filled the bleachers. To their delight, Ruth struck out 22 batters, and St. Mary's won by a final score of 6–0.

One man that was mightily impressed by Ruth's dominant performance was Jack Dunn. Dunn was the owner and manager of the Baltimore Orioles, then a **minor-league** team playing in the International League, one step below the major leagues. Dunn was

Jack Dunn, shown here on a baseball card from 1911, was the owner and manager of the International League's Baltimore Orioles. He watched Babe Ruth's big game against Mount St. Joseph's and eventually offered him a pro contract.

Jack Dunn (1872–1928)

Jack Dunn had been a major-league pitcher, infielder, and outfielder for the Brooklyn Bridegrooms and Superbas, Baltimore Orioles, Philadelphia Phillies, and New York Giants, but he made his biggest impact on baseball as a minor-league manager and owner. Born in Meadville, Pennsylvania, in 1872, Dunn had a poor, four-year major-league pitching career. After hurting his arm, he switched positions to become a good-fielding, poor-hitting infielder. He retired with a .245 lifetime **batting average**.

Known for his knowledge of the game more than his ability, Dunn became the player-manager of the Baltimore Orioles in 1907. The Orioles were a minor-league team with no connection to today's major-league club of the same name. Two years later, he bought the Orioles from owner Ned Hanlon.

With his keen eye for recruiting top talent, Dunn built the Orioles into one of the greatest minor-league clubs in baseball history. Dunn's Orioles won seven consecutive International League championships from 1919 to 1925. Besides Babe Ruth, one of the stars that Dunn signed was Lefty Grove, later a Hall of Fame pitcher with the Philadelphia Athletics and Boston Red Sox.

Dunn owned the Orioles until his death in 1928.

Before Jack Dunn became the owner of the minor-league Baltimore Orioles, he played for several Major League Baseball teams. This photo is from 1902, when he played for the National League's New York Giants.

also a professional baseball scout, meaning that if he signed a player to a contract, he could then sell that player to a major-league club and earn a sizable profit. Dunn was always searching for new talent. He knew Brother Gilbert from hanging around baseball fields and had read newspaper reports about George Ruth. Dunn was curious to see this "speed boy" from the reform school.

After the game, Dunn asked Brother Gilbert to introduce him to Ruth. Dunn told Ruth that he would visit St. Mary's in February to offer Ruth a professional baseball contract, saying that Ruth was "the most promising young ballplayer I've ever seen." George was flabbergasted. He had never considered baseball as a career. His destiny was sewing shirts. Now he had a chance to do what he loved and get paid for it. Play baseball for a living—who would have believed it, he thought. In his autobiography, Ruth said he had reacted this way: "I guess I must have come near falling over in my excitement. Did I want to play baseball? Does a fish like to swim or a squirrel climb trees? I didn't even pause to ask questions. 'Sure,' I said. 'I'll play. When do I start?'"

> *Dunn was curious to see this "speed boy" from the reform school.*

CHAPTER 4

Becoming the Babe

There were moments when I felt on top of the world, and moments when my stomach turned over—wondering if I could make the grade . . .

Jack Dunn arrived at St. Mary's as promised on February 14, 1914. It was St. Valentine's Day, a cold, snowy Saturday, one week after Ruth's nineteenth birthday. Dunn was there to give Ruth a contract to pitch for the Orioles. Only one problem stood in the way: George was too young to sign a legal document. He needed to be twenty-one. Even though Ruth's father was alive and running Ruth's Café in Baltimore, George was still a ward in the custody of the Xaverian Brothers and would remain so until his twenty-first birthday.

Brother Matthias thought of a solution. Mr. Dunn could become George's legal guardian and sign the contract for him. Dunn promised to take good care of his new pitcher, and a week later, on February 22, he signed the papers. Ruth was now a member of the Baltimore Orioles. The news that George had agreed to a contract with the Orioles quickly spread throughout the dormitories of St. Mary's. One proud student was heard to say sadly, "There goes our ball club!"

Five days later, on Friday, February 27, Ruth left St. Mary's. The final note written in the school ledger read: "He is going to join the Baltimore Baseball Team." First,

Babe Ruth (far right) poses with his Baltimore teammates in this photo from 1914. He played for the International League team until July of that year.

George said good-bye to his friends and to the brothers. He saved the final farewell for Brother Matthias, the man who had taught him everything he knew. While George was excited to be leaving St. Mary's, he knew he would miss the brother's guidance and support. They shook hands. "You'll make it, George," Matthias told him.

Leaving Home

With the blessing of Brother Matthias, George Ruth walked out through the gates of St. Mary's as a professional baseball player. He had been instructed by Dunn to catch a train at Baltimore's Union Station on the afternoon of Monday, March 2. From there, he would join a dozen other players heading south for Fayetteville, North Carolina, where the Orioles held **spring training** camp.

With three days to go before leaving town and nowhere to stay, George visited with his father in the apartment above the saloon. His mother had died two years earlier, when he was seventeen. Nobody knows what advice George's father gave him.

"I was 19 and the proudest, greenest [most inexperienced] kid in the country," George crowed.

George Ruth was eager to start a new life, but he was also a bundle of nerves. He had never before set foot outside Baltimore, and he had little understanding of the world except how to sew a shirt and play baseball. More than a foot of snow covered the city's streets, and gale-force

George Ruth was eager to start a new life, but he was also a bundle of nerves.

winds blew roofs off houses on the day George left home. It was Baltimore's worst winter storm in twenty-five years. Through this snowstorm, he made his way to Union Station to board a train. Nothing could keep him from becoming a professional ballplayer.

The train to Fayetteville left Baltimore on schedule in a blizzard. This was George's first time on a train. One of the veteran players, Ben Egan, showed him how to fold down the sleeping berth in his cabin. Two years earlier, Egan had been a major-league catcher for manager Connie Mack's Philadelphia Athletics. As a rookie (a player in his first season), George was grateful to receive a helping hand from an experienced teammate.

However, the veteran players on the team wasted no time in making Ruth the butt of practical jokes and gags. George was naive and easily fooled. When he asked Egan about the purpose of a mesh sling hanging from the ceiling above his cot, Egan told him it was a special hammock-like device for pitchers to rest their arms while sleeping. The mesh hammock was really a place to store clothes, but George had no clue. He spent an uncomfortable and sleepless night with his left arm suspended above his head. By morning he had a stiff shoulder and a sore arm. The gullible rookie pitcher fell for every prank in the book, even wearing his shoes to sleep so that they wouldn't be stolen.

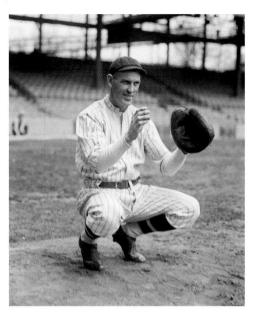

Ben Egan was a veteran player on Baltimore's 1914 team who played a practical joke on rookie Babe Ruth. Egan was also a big-league catcher in four seasons between 1908 and 1915.

Spring Training Antics

In Fayetteville, the team stayed at the Hotel Lafayette. Ruth's biggest thrill was riding the hotel elevator. He had so much fun that he rode up and down for hours, acting like an overgrown child. It also delighted George that he could eat anything he wanted at the team's expense.

Ruth's appetite was legendary. He ordered enormous amounts of food: eighteen-egg omelets with three slabs of ham and six slices of toast; tubs of fried chicken and racks of barbecued ribs; rib roasts, beefsteaks, and pork chops by the pound; and for dessert a whole gallon of ice cream in one sitting. Teammates watched in amazement as he gulped it all down and asked for more. "Anybody who eats three pounds of steak and a bottle of chili sauce for a starter has got me," said a teammate.

Ruth's teammates were entertained by his huge appetite for food and amused by his daring stunts. As a kid in Pigtown, he never owned a bicycle. In Fayetteville, he made friends with some local boys who rode their bicycles to the ballpark. Bike riding looked like fun, so he borrowed a bike and was soon pedaling around town. He liked to ride fast. One day, he came whizzing around a corner and nearly ran over Jack Dunn. Swerving, he skidded the bike to avoid Dunn and violently crashed into a hay wagon. Ruth flew six feet into the air and landed smack on his back, with the bike a twisted pile of metal atop his chest. Dunn stood over the senseless young pitcher and scolded him for such a reckless act.

Ruth flew six feet into the air and landed smack on his back, with the bike a twisted pile of metal atop his chest.

"You want to go back to that school?" Dunn yelled. "You behave yourself, you hear me? You're a ballplayer—not a circus act."

Raw Rookie

Ruth had a taste for adventure. He was raw and unsophisticated. On the field, he was an immediate success. Off the field, he was overwhelmed by a world totally foreign to him. George's innocent but reckless behavior became an inside joke among his teammates, who teased him about it constantly. "There were moments when I felt on top of the world," he would recall, "and moments when my stomach turned over—wondering if I could make the grade and fearful that I'd fail, and be forced to go back to St. Mary's."

Young rookies in those days were razzed and teased by the veteran players without mercy. Ruth was an easy target. But Jack Dunn had made a promise to the brothers that he would be Ruth's protector, and he made sure to keep his promise.

One day, as the teasing reached a boiling point, Orioles coach Sam Steinman warned the players to go easy on the rookie because "he's one of Jack Dunn's babes." In other words, lay off the kid, because he's the manager's favorite pet prospect.

But Jack Dunn had made a promise to the brothers that he would be Ruth's protector, and he made sure to keep his promise.

The players continued to rag Ruth by calling him Dunnie's Babe and then just Babe. A sportswriter from the *Baltimore Sun* picked up on the nickname and used it in his articles. From then on, George Ruth was called Babe Ruth or simply the Babe, even in places where few people had ever heard of baseball.

Colorful Nicknames

In the coming decade, headline writers would refer to Babe Ruth by many colorful nicknames, including the Sultan of Swat, the Bambino (the Italian word for "babe"), the Big Bam, the Behemoth of Bust, the Colossus of Clout, the Maharajah of Mash, the Mastodonic Mauler, the Prince of Pounders, the Rajah of Rap, the Wali of Wallop, and the Wazir of Wham.

Turning Heads

Babe Ruth played his first spring training game with the Orioles at Fayetteville's Cape Fear Fairgrounds on March 7, 1914. In the seventh inning, he did what he would become famous for in ballparks all across the country: he belted a majestic home run. Measured at four hundred feet, the home run was the longest hit ever seen by the local fans. Ruth's ball was hit so far into a cornfield beyond the fairgrounds that Bill Morrisette, playing right field that day, joked that traveling so far to retrieve the ball would require cab fare!

Ruth had hit the longest home run in Fayetteville history in only his fifth day as a professional ballplayer, in his first game ever, and in just his second time at bat. Thirty-eight years later, a man who had been the batboy for that game persuaded Fayetteville officials to put up a marker on the spot honoring Ruth's first home run in professional baseball. Dunn wrote a letter to Brother Gilbert that read, "Brother, this fellow Ruth is the greatest young ballplayer who ever reported to a training camp."

Proud Homecoming

He had left Baltimore in March as George Ruth. One month later, when spring training was over, he returned to the city as Babe Ruth. His contract with the Orioles was paying him $100 a month for the six-month season. Today that would equal more than $2,000 a month. Receiving his first paycheck, he felt like a rich man. George's only experience with money until then was the spare change he stole from his father's cash box and the few coins he earned for candy by sewing shirts. "My jaw must have dropped," he said of the most money he had ever put in his pocket. "It made me as lightheaded as if I had been hit on the head with a bat."

Ruth went out and bought a motorcycle. His first trip on the motorcycle was to St. Mary's. Brother Matthias was there to welcome him inside. George had six tickets to the Orioles' opening-day game, and when he appeared at the ballpark that afternoon, he had six boys from the school with him. Ruth led them to their seats like a proud father and gave each boy spending money for food and souvenirs. Babe Ruth always tried to be an inspiration to kids, especially those kids in need.

The St. Mary's school would continue to operate for thirty-six years after Ruth left, and the story of his troubled beginnings would be told at St. Mary's time and again as a story of hope.

Ruth, who never forgot his days at St. Mary's, had a soft spot for needy kids for the rest of his life. He signs baseballs for this group of enthusiastic youngsters in New York in 1927.

CHAPTER 5

From Baltimore to Boston

*Going to the Red Sox was a great break.
In those days the Red Sox were [the] kings
of the baseball walk.*

The Baltimore Orioles were a team in the International League, a minor league that still exists today. Baltimore had lost its own Major League Baseball team in 1903, when the Orioles moved to New York as the Highlanders (later to become the Yankees). The minor-league Orioles were going strong until 1914, when a new major league, called the Federal League, placed a team in Baltimore. The owner of Baltimore's new major-league team, the Terrapins, was Ned Hanlon, the former major-league Orioles owner. Hanlon built a new stadium across the street from where

The Baltimore Orioles were one of baseball's top franchises in the late 1890s. This photo is from 1898, when the team won 96 games and finished in second place in the National League.

The Federal League

Baseball had become such a profitable business by 1914 that a third professional league, the Federal League, declared itself a major league, and its eight owners began buying star ballplayers from the National League and American League.

On April 13, 1914, one day before opening day for the two other major leagues, the Federal League launched its inaugural season as the host Baltimore Terrapins beat the Buffalo Feds 3–2 in front of 27,140 spectators. American League and National League officials took notice of the large crowd. Months earlier, they had decided to take the new league to court to stop it from stealing their star players.

The Federal League, hounded by lawsuits from the other two leagues, soon began losing money. Fans, their curiosity satisfied, returned to watching the established American League and National League teams. A year later, the Federal League folded. No rival baseball league has since competed against the American and National Leagues.

the minor-league Orioles played. This was bad news for Jack Dunn and the Orioles.

The idea of being a major-league city again energized Baltimore. Everyone was talking about the Terrapins, the Federal League, and the return of big-league baseball to Baltimore.

Poor Attendance

Babe Ruth made his formal debut as a Baltimore professional when he took the mound at Oriole Park against the Buffalo Bisons on April 22, 1914. He pitched a shutout—a

complete-game victory allowing no runs for the opposing team—
and he also got 2 hits. It was a memorable performance for
the local boy, a rookie pitching as a pro for the first time in his
hometown. Yet fewer than two hundred fans witnessed Ruth's
first game in Baltimore. Ten times
that number were sitting across the
street at Terrapin Park.

*It was a memorable
performance for the local
boy, a rookie pitching as
a pro for the first time in
his hometown.*

The poor attendance at Orioles
games continued throughout the first
few weeks of the season. In early
May, the Orioles were in second place
in the International League, but the
Terrapins were in first place in the Federal League. The local
papers didn't even bother to send a writer along with Dunn's
team on its first road trip.

When it became obvious that Ruth was a splendid talent,
Dunn upped Ruth's salary in May to $200 a month and then
raised it again in June to $300 a month. Ruth had more money
than he knew how to spend. Dunn, on the other hand, was
losing money—lots of it. The Orioles were a good team, but
they were still a minor-league team. Fans preferred to watch the
upstart Terrapins, a major-league team, play.

Dunn's Difficult Decision

The Orioles couldn't compete with the Terrapins on a level
playing field. Business got so bad that when Ruth pitched five
innings to beat a Toronto team on June 25, with only nineteen
fans in the stands, the vendors went across the street to Terrapin
Park in search of paying customers. In July, the Orioles won 13
games in a row to surge into first place. Ruth had won 14 of the
20 games he pitched and was hitting home runs whenever he

connected (successfully hit the ball). But nobody in Baltimore seemed to notice or care. The Orioles were close to bankruptcy, and Dunn needed to take action. By early July, he had no choice but to sell his best players to major-league teams in order to raise enough money to pay his bills.

Ruth, catcher Ben Egan, and pitcher Ernie Shore were called into Jack Dunn's office on July 9 and told of their sale to the Boston Red Sox. Egan and Shore were excited to leave Baltimore and play for a major-league team, but Ruth begged Dunn to keep him. Ruth wanted to stay in Baltimore, and he was loyal to Dunn. The owner explained to Ruth that a big-league team was where he belonged. Boston spent the hefty sum of $25,000 to purchase the three players, but Ruth was the main player they wanted in the deal. Boston immediately gave its new young left-hander a starting salary of $625 a month. Nine other players were sold by Dunn to other teams at bargain prices. With their best players now in the majors, the Orioles would topple quickly and finish the season in sixth place.

Major-League Rookie

Four months after leaving Baltimore in a blizzard on the first train ride of his life, Babe Ruth was on his way to the big leagues to play for the Boston Red Sox. "Going to the Red Sox was a great break," he would later say. "In those days the Red Sox were [the] kings of the baseball walk."

Ruth arrived by train at Boston's Back Bay Station on the morning of July 11, 1914. Later that afternoon, he was pitching for the Red Sox and winning his first big-league game 4–3 against the Cleveland Indians at Fenway Park. Relying mostly on his fastball, Ruth pitched fiercely, and Cleveland's batters managed a mere 8 **singles** over the course of seven innings.

Babe Ruth got his first look at Fenway Park in the summer of 1914, when the American League's Boston Red Sox bought his contract. This is how the ballpark, which had been built in 1912, looked that year.

Young and brimming with confidence, the pushy rookie pitcher who liked to hit took his turn in batting practice with the regular Red Sox players the next day. His teammates viewed this as unacceptable behavior from an unproven rookie. Rookies always take batting practice as a group to keep them in their place. Besides, Ruth was there to pitch, not hit. The next day, Ruth came to his locker to discover that some teammates had neatly sawed all his bats in two.

The message was clear. Ruth was just another rookie from the minors, joining a team that already had many star players. The outfield of Tris Speaker, Harry Hooper, and Duffy Lewis was among the best of all time. The Red Sox had opened brand-new Fenway Park with a World Series title in 1912, and many of the players from that team remained.

This baseball from the Hall of Fame is signed by the legendary Tris Speaker, who played in the big leagues from 1907 to 1928. He was not only one of the greatest hitters ever, but also one of the finest defensive outfielders.

Seeking Acceptance

For the second time in the same season, Ruth was a newcomer to his team. Soon after arriving in Boston, he found a rooming house on Batavia Street and met a waitress at Landers Coffee Shop. Babe would eat there a lot and flirt with the pretty sixteen-year-old waitress named Helen Woodford. Ruth was enjoying life, dating Helen, and spending money as fast as he got it.

With a deep pitching staff of Smoky Joe Wood, Ray Collins, Dutch Leonard, and Rube Foster turning in great seasons for the Red Sox, it would be difficult for a new pitcher to break in with the ball club. Ruth had earned his first major-league victory, but he did not impress his new manager, Bill Carrigan, who also served as the team's catcher. Ruth's second chance to pitch in the major leagues came the following week against the Detroit Tigers, but he failed miserably and was removed from the game by his manager in the fourth inning. The Tigers' batters feasted on Ruth's curveball, as if they knew that the pitch was coming. Carrigan didn't let the young left-hander play for nearly a month, and then in August of that season, Ruth was sent to a minor-league team in Providence, Rhode Island.

Being sent down to the minor leagues was a blow to Babe's ego. The move forty miles south to Providence took Ruth away from Helen, though he did find a way to return to Boston to see her as often as he could. He also met other women at the many parties he attended. Having been confined for so many years at St. Mary's, Ruth was making up for lost time. "He didn't drink when he came to Boston," outfielder Harry Hooper said, "and I don't think he'd ever been with a woman." But once Ruth was exposed to dating and drinking, he never could get enough.

Finding Providence

Now standing six feet two inches and weighing 190 pounds, Ruth was a hard thrower with a decent curveball to go with his fastball. He had talent but was not a finished product. He had a bad habit of tipping off batters to his pitches by curling his tongue out of the corner of his mouth when he would throw a curve. If a hitter knows a certain type of pitch is coming, he has a huge advantage. Providence manager "Wild Bill" Donovan quickly helped to cure Ruth of that habit.

Over the next six weeks, Ruth won nine games. His contributions helped Providence reach the top of the International League standings. Due to his good performance on the Providence team, he got the order to come back to Boston to pitch a game at the end of the season. He beat the New York Yankees on October 2 and got his first hit for the Red Sox, a **double** off pitcher King Cole. Babe Ruth's first year in professional baseball had come to an end. He had

Babe is pictured here in the uniform of the Providence Grays in 1914. He was sent down to the minor-league club not long after making his big-league debut with the Red Sox that year.

received one fan letter, from Brother Matthias. It read, "You're doing fine, George. I'm proud of you."

The boy who back in March had never before set foot outside Baltimore had now lived in three different cities and played for three different teams. He had grown accustomed to train travel and hotel elevators. He got his first driver's license and bought a new suit. He picked finely tailored silk shirts, all monogrammed GHR. Most gentlemen of the day wore a brimmed hat, but the Babe liked to wear a flat camel's-hair cap, which was not the fashion, but he didn't care. He flaunted his own unique style, and he was in a class by himself.

But Ruth was not alone when he returned to Baltimore after the 1914 season. He came home with Helen Woodford, the Boston waitress from

He flaunted his own unique style, and he was in a class by himself.

Landers Coffee Shop. In late September, the Babe asked Helen to marry him. She said yes. On October 17, 1914, they were married in St. Paul's Catholic Church in Ellicott City, a small town just west of Baltimore. Babe was almost twenty; Helen had just turned seventeen. Helen's parents thought they were too young to get married. They had known each other three months, and for much of that time, Babe had been away from Boston. There was no honeymoon. They spent the winter in a room above the saloon where Babe tended bar with his father. Big

Babe Ruth and Helen Woodford were married in October 1914. This photograph was taken in their first year of marriage.

George had remarried, and Babe and Helen helped him and his new wife tend bar in the family tavern.

CHAPTER 6

Pitching for a Living

I didn't think much of becoming a slugger. I liked to hit . . . But it was pitching which took my time in Boston.

Since his parents had mistakenly told him he had been born in 1894, Babe Ruth believed he had turned twenty-one in February 1915. He was a married man, a professional ballplayer, and now legally freed as the ward of the brothers of St. Mary's and from his guardian, Jack Dunn. A month later, he left Helen behind in Baltimore and reported to the Red Sox spring training camp in Hot Springs, Arkansas, ready to crack Boston's deep starting pitching staff.

Although still immature and inexperienced, Ruth was a far cry from the overwhelmed boy he had been when he had arrived in Fayetteville for spring training the year before. There, he was the butt of jokes, but in Hot Springs,

Ruth reported to his first spring training with the Red Sox in 1915 ready to compete for a spot on the team's pitching staff. He made the club and went on to win 18 games for the World Series champs.

he was oozing with confidence, and he would turn the tables on his teammates. He nailed shoes to the floor. He punched holes in the tops of straw hats. He slipped sheets of cardboard into sandwiches.

"People sometimes got mad at him, . . . but I never heard of anybody who didn't like Babe Ruth."

Though not all the players enjoyed being around him, he was a fun-loving, overenthusiastic presence, and the majority of players accepted the second-year pitcher as you would a mischievous little brother. "People sometimes got mad at him," said teammate Bob Shawkey, "but I never heard of anybody who didn't *like* Babe Ruth."

One Down, 713 to Go

Babe Ruth was the starting pitcher against the New York Yankees on May 6, 1915, and though the Red Sox lost that day 4–3, Ruth hit a pitch thrown by Jack Warhop into the right-field stands of the Polo Grounds, where the Yankees played their home games. It was the first of what would eventually become 714 career home runs. At the time he hit it, however, few could imagine such an amazing future.

When the Red Sox returned to New York in early June, Ruth again socked a mighty homer into the right-field grandstand, this one longer and higher than the first. To avoid further damage against his team, "Wild Bill" Donovan, who had been Ruth's skipper at Providence and was now managing the Yankees, employed an unconventional tactic in Ruth's next two plate appearances. Both times, Donovan ordered that Ruth be given an intentional **walk**; even though it meant putting Ruth on base, it took away the chance of Ruth hitting a home run. Donovan's strategy raised eyebrows. This was the time in baseball's history known as the Dead Ball Era, when offense was scarce. The fans were upset each time Ruth was purposely passed to first base; they wanted to see him hit. Until Ruth began hitting so many home runs, baseball was a game in which runs were usually scored one at a time by bunching singles together. Home runs were not unheard-of, but, until this time, they had been few and far between. Ruth's barrage of power soon would transform the game, making it possible to defeat an opponent with one mighty swing of the bat.

This photo of "Wild Bill" Donovan is from 1915, when he was the manager of the Yankees. That year, Donovan started the unconventional practice of walking Ruth intentionally in some situations.

Rough Edges

Ruth's pitching and hitting amazed his teammates, but his personal habits concerned them. He was vulgar and crude and used very poor language. The pitcher Ernie Shore, one of Ruth's roommates on team road trips, could not stand living with him. According to Shore, Ruth regularly walked around naked, constantly passed gas and belched loudly, never flushed the toilet, never sat down, never went to sleep, and had the distressing habit of wearing the same underwear day after day. When Shore complained about Ruth using his toothbrush, Ruth waved him away and said, "That's all right, Ernie, I'm not particular."

Dead Ball Era

From 1900 to 1919, baseball was dominated by great pitchers such as Cy Young, Walter Johnson, Christy Mathewson, and Grover Cleveland Alexander. Good pitching and speed on the base paths were the marks of the best teams. During those years, players such as Frank "Home Run" Baker, who hit 10 to 12 homers in a season, led the league. Runs were created through **bunting**, short hits, and **stealing**.

This period took its name of the Dead Ball Era from the baseball itself. In those days, the baseball was softer. The many layers of wool inside the leather covers were more loosely wound. The baseballs didn't travel that far even when batters managed to hit them hard. Also, pitchers at this time were allowed to smear the ball with dirt or tobacco juice. They were allowed to scuff, use sandpaper on, or spit on the ball. Because of this, the ball moved in an unpredictable manner and could be difficult to see as it crossed the plate. There were some great hitters during those years—Ty Cobb, "Shoeless" Joe Jackson, Honus Wagner, and Nap Lajoie all had career batting averages well over .300—but the pitchers had a clear advantage.

Baseball was a different game in the Dead Ball Era. In this photo, spectators in Detroit line the outfield to watch a World Series game between the hometown Tigers and the Chicago Cubs.

The Babe also had trouble remembering names throughout his life. He didn't remember the names of most teammates, much less the opposition. Anyone younger than Babe was named Kid, pronounced "keed." Anyone older than Babe was called Doc. The Babe's problem remembering names embarrassed him. "I can remember every ball ever pitched to me, but names don't stick," he said.

Teammates sometimes called him Jidge, a New England pronunciation for "George," but opponents teased him with such less pleasant names as Big Baboon, Tarzan, and Ape Man. Of course, no one dared speak these names to his face. At six feet two inches and 215 pounds, Ruth was one of the biggest and strongest men in baseball. He used a heavy bat weighing fifty-two ounces. Most bats today weigh about thirty-two ounces. He was strong enough to swing it and believed that the weight of the bat made the balls he hit travel farther.

Ruth, who swung a very heavy bat, was known for his immense strength. In this photo from the 1920s, he's carrying a log that reportedly weighed three hundred pounds.

Married Strangers

With Babe's salary now boosted to $3,500 per year, he and Helen moved into an apartment in Cambridge, Massachusetts, near Harvard University. Helen set up house, but Babe rarely stayed home. He went out most nights in search of a party and often found exactly what he was looking for. Helen, however, was shy and awkward around other people. She was often uncomfortable, an outsider, unable to relate to the other baseball players and their wives. She did not understand Babe's popularity and was surprised when people recognized him on the street.

Babe Ruth was in a comfortable position with the Red Sox. He was making lots of money, and he enjoyed spending it. When the team arrived in a new city, Ruth would drop his suitcase off in his hotel room and immediately go out for the night drinking, gambling, and looking for women. A reporter once asked Ping Bodie what it was like to be Babe Ruth's roommate on these trips. "I don't room with him," said Bodie. "I room with his suitcase."

Babe's fame had made him popular with the many women he would encounter, at home and on the road. Parties lasted deep into the early morning hours, and he often showed up for games having had little or no sleep. Yet as his behavior got worse, his play got better and better. He somehow seemed immune from the effects that such bad habits would have on most people. He could party all night and still pitch well and hit a home run in the game the next afternoon.

"To understand him," said teammate Joe Dugan, "you had to understand this: He wasn't human."

World Series Snub

Babe Ruth finished his first full major-league season with a record of 18 wins and 8 losses and a 2.44 **earned run average**

(ERA). He also had a .315 batting average with 4 home runs in just 92 at bats. The American League home run leader had 7 home runs. Since a pitcher gets fewer at bats than a regular-position player who plays most every game (starting pitchers pitch only every four or five games), by comparison, Ruth's home run output was impressive. Had he not continued as a pitcher for the next three years, he might have hit another 100 home runs and put his career home run record beyond the reach of everybody. However, Ruth was one of the best left-handed pitchers in the league, and he and the Red Sox still saw his future as a pitcher.

"In the Red Sox days, I didn't think much of becoming a slugger," he said. "I liked to hit. All fellows do. There isn't a man in baseball today who isn't happiest when he's up there at the plate with a stick in his hand. But it was pitching which took my time in Boston."

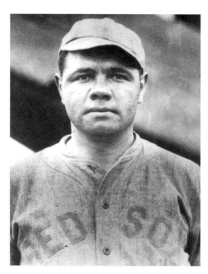

Ruth played for the Red Sox from 1914 through 1919. In that time, he established a reputation as one of the best left-handed pitchers in the American League.

The 1915 **pennant**-winning Red Sox had many good pitchers. Ruth was one of five to win at least 15 games that season. In the World Series against the Philadelphia Phillies, won by the Red Sox in 5 games, manager Bill Carrigan never called on Ruth to throw a single pitch. The Babe's services just weren't needed, his manager had decided. "I ate my heart out on the bench in that Series," said Ruth. "I grabbed Carrigan's lapels before every game and demanded to know when I was to get my chance." As good as Ruth was, he was still a young player, and the veteran manager chose to send his more experienced players to the field.

When the Series was over, Ruth's frustration was soothed somewhat by the $3,780 winner's share he received for being a member of the world-championship team. The bonus check was $280 more than his entire year's salary and pushed his earnings for the season up to nearly $7,500. This was in a time when new cars cost a few hundred dollars! Babe returned to Baltimore for the winter. With the extra money, he bought his father a new bar at the corner of Lombard and Eutaw streets, and then worked there until it was time for the 1916 season to begin.

World Series Star

In 1916, only his second full season in the majors, Ruth, age twenty-one, became the leader of the Red Sox's pitching staff. He won 23 games and led the American League with a 1.75 earned run average and 9 **shutouts**, an American League record for left-handers that wouldn't be matched for sixty-two years. He also hit 3 home runs, tied for best on the team.

The Red Sox won their third American League pennant in five seasons and their second in a row. In the World Series, the Red Sox faced the Brooklyn Dodgers. Boston won Game One at

Ruth led the American League in shutouts and ERA in 1916. In this photo from that year, he sits in the dugout with manager Bill Carrigan (second from left) and teammates Jack Barry (second from right) and Vean Gregg (far right).

home 6–5. The second game of the Series, also played in Boston, was a pitchers' duel between Brooklyn's Sherry Smith and Ruth, who finally made it into the World Series as a pitcher. (He had batted once, but not pitched, in the previous year's Series.)

Ruth's performance in this game cemented his reputation as a great pitcher. In the first inning, a Brooklyn hitter scored on an inside-the-park home run. Ruth evened the score himself two innings later, hitting into a **groundout** that scored a run. At the end of nine innings the score was still tied, so the game went into extra innings. Finally, in the bottom of the fourteenth inning, the Red Sox scored the winning run for a 2–1 victory. After allowing that first home run, the remainder of the game was a shutout, with Ruth pitching thirteen innings and setting a Series single-game record.

In the clubhouse afterward, he grabbed Carrigan in a bear hug and, never one to hold a grudge, yelled joyfully at his manager, "I told you a year ago I could take care of those National League bums."

The city of Boston celebrated its second World Series triumph in a row, and Ruth had become the most dominant left-handed pitcher in baseball. He received another winner's share, this time for $3,910, and with the money bought an eighty-acre farm in Sudbury, Massachusetts, about twenty-five miles from Boston. He named it Home Plate Farm. There, he relaxed by fishing, hunting, and chopping wood. Helen wanted to make the farm a permanent home, but her husband found the country life too quiet to stay around very long. There was too much fun to be had in the city, and to the Babe, it seemed that the fun was never ending.

Babe Ruth works on his farm in Sudbury, Massachusetts. Helen Ruth wanted to make the quiet farm their permanent home, but Babe was drawn to the excitement of the big city.

CHAPTER 7

The Changing World

I'll win more games playing every day in the outfield than I will pitching every fourth day.

Baseball was poised to start a new season when the United States formally entered World War I on April 6, 1917. Thousands of Americans—and some baseball players—answered the recruiting call from their **Uncle Sam** and enlisted to fight for the Allied forces. The most famous major-league players, like Babe Ruth, were not called to war in 1917. The following year, however, things changed. In 1918, baseball players became subject to the military draft unless they were working in a job that helped support the war effort, like shipbuilding or arms manufacturing.

The war took a toll on every part of American life, including sports. A number of major sporting events were canceled, including

This is Ruth's registration card from 1917 for the military draft. Although the United States officially entered World War I in April of that year, Babe was not called into the service.

The Great War

On April 6, 1917, the United States declared war on Germany. The United States had formally entered a war that had begun in 1914 between German and Austro-Hungarian forces and those of European allies such as Great Britain, France, Belgium, and others. The United States joined on the side of Great Britain and its allies to battle German-led forces. The entry of the United States into this battle made it the First World War, also called the Great War.

On June 1, 1917, about two months after the United States formally entered World War I, Boston Braves catcher Hank Gowdy, a hero of the 1914 World Series, joined the Ohio National Guard, becoming the first major leaguer to enlist in the service.

Hank Gowdy (in military uniform, saluting) was the first Major League Baseball player to enlist in the service during World War I. Gowdy, who played for the Boston Braves, is shown here posing with the Giants' Jack Onslow before a World Series game in 1917.

the Indianapolis 500 auto race and golf's U.S. Open. College football selected no All-America team. Even so, baseball was able to continue. But baseball, it turned out, would not be immune to war, either. During the war years, professional baseball would suffer from both lack of players and lack of fans.

Almost Perfect

Babe Ruth was a returning World Series hero and the opening-day starter for the 1917 season. Tensions erupted on June 23, when one of the strangest games in baseball began with Ruth pitching. He must have been in an irritable mood that afternoon when he took the mound against the Washington Senators at Boston's Fenway Park. Each of his first three pitches to the Senators leadoff batter Ray Morgan was called a **ball**.

Ruth did not like the calls and left the mound to argue with umpire Brick Owens. Ruth's fourth pitch was called ball four. An infuriated Ruth went berserk and was ejected from the game. He then approached home plate and punched Owens in the jaw. For that, Ruth was suspended for ten days and fined $100. "It wasn't a love pat," said Ruth. "I really socked him."

Red Sox pitcher Ernie Shore came in to replace Ruth. After Morgan was thrown out while trying to steal second base, Shore then induced outs from the next 26 Washington batters in a row. For many years, the baseball records said that Shore had pitched a perfect game—one of baseball's rarest feats in which no batter reaches base safely. Not including Shore's, only 18 such games have ever been pitched in the majors in more than 125 years. In 1991, a new rule said that a perfect game must be a game in which no batter ever reaches base. Because of the batter Ruth walked, Shore's name was taken off the list.

Ruth and Red Sox teammate Ernie Shore (right) are forever linked in baseball lore because of a game in 1917. Babe walked the first hitter, then was thrown out of the game. Shore relieved him and did not allow another batter to reach base.

Ruth's outburst was an example of self-discipline problems that would become personal obstacles throughout his career. Although there was no doubt that Babe belonged in the big leagues, in many ways he was still a rough kid from the waterfront. He was often fined and suspended for losing his temper, and he fought frequently with his managers because he regularly broke team rules by staying out too late.

A Bold Idea

Ruth had another outstanding season on the mound in 1917, winning 24 games with a 2.01 ERA and 6 shutouts. But the lasting memory of that season was a long-distance home run that he hit. It was the first ever struck into the deepest center-field bleachers at Fenway Park. Pitchers are not usually known for their hitting skills, and even though Ruth was still a few years away from making his name as a hitter, he was becoming known for his ability to hit the ball a great distance. "The more I see of Babe," said Boston sportswriter Burt Whitman, "the more he seems a figure out of mythology."

The Red Sox finished the 1917 season in second place, behind the eventual World Series champion Chicago White Sox. In the off-season, Ruth met with the team's new owner, Harry Frazee, and suggested he would be more valuable as

Harry Frazee was the owner of the Boston Red Sox from 1916 to 1923. Although often criticized as the man who sold Babe Ruth to the Yankees, Frazee earlier convinced manager Ed Barrow to play his star pitcher in the outfield—even if it was only to sell more tickets.

an everyday player. Instead of just pitching, he could play outfield, too, giving him more chances to hit. "I'll win more games playing every day in the outfield than I will pitching every fourth day," he said.

Harry Frazee was a theatrical producer. A showman, Frazee noticed that when Ruth was on the mound, the Red Sox drew large crowds. What might they do if Ruth played every day? Frazee pressed new manager Ed Barrow to convert Ruth from a pitcher to an outfielder. Barrow refused. Ruth had hit 9 home runs in four American League seasons, but he was the best young left-handed pitcher in the league. Barrow worried that he would be viewed as a laughingstock if he put Ruth in the outfield. Pitching was the most important feature of the game, and left-handed pitching was the hardest of all baseball talents to find and develop. Barrow let Ruth play a little in the outfield and at first base during spring training games, but he let it be known that pitching was going to be Ruth's job when the season started. Ruth let it be known that he liked to hit.

Late-Night Stunts

The war had forced many roster changes by the start of the 1918 season, as thirteen Red Sox players were called for military duty. Because he was short on players, Barrow played Ruth in the outfield on the days he did not pitch. That solved one problem for the moment, but Ruth continued to create more.

Ruth's off-the-field behavior would be a major problem for his manager in 1918. In August, Babe's father had died outside the saloon that Babe had bought for him. Someone punched Big George, and he lost his balance. He fell, hitting his head on the pavement. Babe was only twenty-three years old, and he had lost both parents. Now he really was an orphan like people always had believed, and he rarely saw his eighteen-year-old sister, Mamie.

That tragedy, plus Ruth's natural interest in late nights, made Barrow worry that Ruth was not getting enough sleep. He tried to rein in Ruth, but rules seldom worked. On the road, Barrow would sit in the hotel lobby until Ruth was in for the night. But he soon found himself losing sleep waiting up for Ruth. One night in Washington, Barrow arranged to have the hotel room next to Ruth. Barrow asked a hotel employee to call him when Babe returned.

At 6:00 a.m., Barrow was awoken and told that Babe had just come in. Storming into Ruth's room, Barrow found the slugger laying innocently in bed, smoking a pipe, the sheets pulled up under his chin. Barrow grabbed the covers and pulled them back, revealing Ruth still fully dressed, shoes and all.

Barrow grabbed the covers and pulled them back, revealing Ruth still fully dressed, shoes and all.

That afternoon, the manager called a team meeting to discuss training rules, aiming most of his talk at Ruth. Fuming and embarrassed, Ruth threatened to punch his manager in the nose. The fifty-year-old Barrow did not back down. A fight was avoided only when teammates stepped in.

Ruth and manager Ed Barrow (seated, left) didn't always see eye to eye. In this photo before the 1918 season, though, they met, along with owner Harry Frazee (seated, right) and infielder Stuffy McInnis (standing, right). The two players were there to sign contracts for that year.

Barrow made Ruth apologize in front of the whole team and made Ruth promise to write a note to Barrow confessing what time he had gotten in the night before.

1918: Champions Again

The war effort had changed Americans' daily life. Due to an order from the Secretary of War that required all ballplayers to be working in wartime industries by September 1, the 1918 schedule was shortened from 154 games to 125. Ruth pitched in 20 games and won 13 times for the Red Sox in the war-shortened 1918 season. He also played outfield in 59 games and first base in 13 games, but he still wasn't playing every game. In only 317 at bats, well below a normal number of at bats for an everyday player, Ruth hit a league-leading 11 home runs. It was the first of twelve times he would lead the league in home runs. Ruth's hitting propelled the Red Sox to another World Series triumph in 1918, this time over the Chicago Cubs.

The new home run champion reminded everyone of his great pitching ability by throwing a 1–0 shutout in the opening game of the Series. Ruth's complete-game shutout, added to his thirteen scoreless innings from two seasons earlier in the 1916 World Series, gave him twenty-two consecutive scoreless innings pitched in the Series. After winning Game Four with seven scoreless innings in his next Series appearance, he had reached twenty-nine straight scoreless innings, a World Series record that would stand for forty-three years. Ruth would often say it was his proudest accomplishment in baseball, greater than any of his batting feats.

One of the other historical highlights of the 1918 Series occurred during the seventh-inning stretch of Game One, when a military band played "The Star-Spangled Banner," which was not yet the national anthem (that did not happen until 1931). Eventually, with the introduction of the public address systems and the outbreak of World War II in 1941, singing the national anthem became the custom before each game.

World War I ended in November 1918. For Boston baseball fans, the future looked bright. The Red Sox had won another championship, the team's third triumph in four years. As things turned out, it was the team's high-water mark for decades. The Red Sox would not win another World Series for eighty-six years.

Fearing Gamblers

For the 1919 season, Babe Ruth was moved to the outfield and pitched less often for the Red Sox. Ruth was thrilled; he was

Ruth is shown pictured here in 1919, his final year with the Red Sox. He belted a big-league-record 29 home runs—an unheard-of total at the time—that season.

losing interest in pitching and wanted to be out there hitting every day. That season, he hit .322 and set a single-season record with 29 home runs. The major leaguer with the next highest home run total that year hit only 12. Ruth's power stunned the baseball world. Nobody had ever hit so many home runs, and few believed it could be done again. Taking his show on the road, Ruth hit a home run in every city in the American League.

However, neither Babe Ruth's home runs nor his 9 pitching wins could lift the Red Sox past the American League champion Chicago White Sox. The Bostonians finished a catastrophic season in sixth place. In the World Series, baseball experts expected the White Sox to have little trouble beating the Cincinnati Reds, but the Reds stunned everyone by winning the Series. Some fans and writers noticed that during the Series, some of Chicago's top players made surprising pitching, fielding, and hitting mistakes.

Rumors swirled that a few of the White Sox players had taken money in exchange for not playing their best so that bettors could be assured the underdog Reds would win. This later became known as the "Black Sox" scandal. Baseball team owners and league officials were concerned. Even the slightest hint of gamblers' involvement would confirm the public's suspicion that baseball did not have an honest image. Owners feared the game was in danger of being destroyed. They needed to turn to someone who would clean things up. The owners grew so worried that fans would lose faith in the game's integrity that they hired a federal judge named Kenesaw Mountain Landis to become baseball's first commissioner. Strong leadership was needed to put the game of baseball back on its feet. As baseball's boss, he and Babe Ruth would team up to help baseball recover from what would be its worst

Star Chicago White Sox pitcher Eddie Cicotte is shown warming up before a game in 1919. Cicotte, who won a league-leading 29 games that season, eventually became a central figure in the infamous "Black Sox" scandal.

scandal yet. Landis would make sure to keep unsavory characters away from the game while Ruth's home runs would generate newspaper headlines and greater fan interest in the sport.

Kenesaw Mountain Landis

Baseball owners were already familiar with Judge Kenesaw Mountain Landis when they turned to him in 1920. The U.S. district court judge, named for a famous Civil War battle, had earned the admiration of the owners when he delayed and then dismissed a lawsuit brought against them by the rival Federal League in 1915.

When Landis became baseball's first commissioner in 1920, he replaced the three-man National Commission that had ruled baseball since 1903. Within his first year as commissioner, Landis had banned a total of fifteen players for breaking league rules. Landis uncovered bribery, thrown games (players losing on purpose), betting plots, and other schemes that showed just how widespread corruption had become in professional baseball.

Landis held the office of commissioner until his death in 1944. He dealt out strict punishment to players, owners, gamblers, and umpires—anyone who showed even a hint of any type of shady behavior. Baseball has had eight commissioners since Judge Landis, but none who wielded so much power.

Judge Kenesaw Mountain Landis is pictured here in 1924. Landis, a former U.S. district court judge, was hired as baseball's first commissioner to salvage the sport's reputation in the aftermath of the "Black Sox" scandal.

CHAPTER 8

Babe's Big Move

If my home run hitting established a new era in baseball . . . that's all the epitaph I want.

Certain dates live in people's memories as unforgettable— even when the occasion is not a happy one. For Red Sox fans, one of those is January 5, 1920. On that day, Boston owner Harry Frazee sold Babe Ruth to the Yankees for $125,000 in cash and a $300,000 loan. It remains the darkest day in team history. Their best player left at the height of his powers and moved to a team that would become a decades-long rival.

Frazee had his reasons, but Red Sox fans didn't care. He owed lots of money to other people and also wanted money to invest in a new Broadway play. He found willing buyers in the Yankees, who were looking for a way to gain attention in the nation's biggest city.

Ruth took advantage of his place as baseball's biggest star. When he joined the Yankees, he demanded—and got—twice as much money as he had been

No, No, Nanette was the Broadway musical that Red Sox owner Harry Frazee helped finance with his sale of Babe Ruth to the New York Yankees. The musical was a rousing success—and soon, so were the Yankees.

paid in Boston. Yankees owners Jacob Ruppert and Tillinghast Huston doubled Ruth's salary to the then-unheard-of amount of $20,000 a year. No athlete had ever been paid so much. But the Babe was worth every penny. His home run hitting would lead the Yankees to seven World Series in fifteen years. Red Sox fans could only curse their bad luck.

The sale of Ruth became the single most important—and infamous—deal in sports history. It dramatically reversed the World Series fortunes of both teams. In 1920, the Yankees were a nineteen-year-old team that had never won a pennant. The Red Sox had won four World Series in the past eight seasons. Ruth, only twenty-five, had already led the American League in home runs. The Yankees would win twenty-six World Series by the end of the century, becoming the most successful team in professional sports.

The Red Sox didn't even play in another World Series until 1946, and the team would not win a World Series for eighty-six years, often failing in heartbreaking fashion. Many fans believed it was Ruth's hex upon them. The phrase "the Curse of the Bambino" became popular following a 1990 book by the same title by *Boston Globe* sports columnist Dan Shaughnessy. This phrase meant that the Boston team was cursed by selling its greatest player to an enemy team.

Home Run Champion

The Yankees decided to permanently make Babe Ruth a right fielder and let him take his swings as a hitter in every game. He would be a hitter, not a pitcher. Now the Babe would really come into his own. In 1920, Ruth once again set a new home run standard that no one thought could ever be topped. He knocked 54 out of the park in a year in which nobody else hit

Ruth is shown batting for the Yankees in 1920. His first season in New York was also his first as a full-time outfielder, and he shattered his own big-league record by hitting 54 home runs.

more than 19. Babe alone smashed more homers than any other *team* in the league! Yet amazingly, the man they were now calling the Sultan of Swat did even better, belting a mind-boggling 59 homers in 1921 to break the single-season record for the third year in a row.

Ruth was a great power hitter, but he had a little help. Two changes in baseball rules and equipment played a small part in his ability to hit home runs. First, the American and National Leagues began using a new brand of baseball. The yarn within the new type of ball itself was wound more tightly. This made the ball harder. The harder ball traveled farther, making home runs more frequent. Second, spitballs—a pitch delivered after the ball has been moistened with saliva or sweat, causing the ball to dart and veer, making it nearly impossible to hit—were outlawed. In addition, baseballs used in games were changed often by the umpire instead of being used until they fell apart. A clean, tightly wound baseball now crossed the plate regularly, and batters could see it better and hit it farther. The era of the pitcher was ending, and the era of the home run hitter was about to begin. Ruth was in the right place at just the right time.

While Ruth gained continued attention for his hitting, the events of the previous year's World Series began to get more headlines. By the summer of 1920, it was clear that something fishy had happened during the 1919 World Series. In September, it was revealed that seven White Sox players—including star pitcher Eddie Cicotte and hitting sensation "Shoeless" Joe Jackson—had accepted bribes from gamblers to intentionally lose the Series. One other player, Buck Weaver, had refused to accept money or throw games, but knew the conspiracy was being planned and failed to inform the authorities. The team had already been known as the Black Sox for their infrequently laundered uniforms, but now the nickname took on a darker connotation. Baseball fans were outraged, and the sport itself was in deep trouble. Baseball's integrity and future faced a very dire threat. Though a court found them not guilty, Judge Landis knew better. He banned all eight from baseball for life. His harsh punishment began the healing process between baseball and its fans. Ruth, it turned out, played a big part in that, too.

Savior of the Game

During the 1921 season, Ruth hit his 139th career home run, surpassing Roger Connor's mark and becoming baseball's all-time leading home run hitter. Ruth, only twenty-six years old and in just his eighth major-league season, was already the game's greatest slugger. Fans came to the ballpark just to catch a glimpse of him. When he took batting practice, opposing players stopped their own preparations to watch his every move.

Ruth crosses home plate after hitting a home run early in the 1921 season. He had a prodigious year at the plate, batting .378 with 59 home runs and 171 runs batted in.

Babe Ruth was evolving into an individual with great public appeal. When the game was still reeling from the "Black Sox" scandal, and when the fans had lost faith in the national pastime, it took a moonfaced kid from Baltimore and his incredible home run swing to restore the nation's love of the game. For this, history looks on Babe Ruth as the "savior" of baseball. His feats gave fans something new to cheer for at a time when things looked bleak.

"If my home run hitting established a new era in baseball,

Babe's towering blasts were awe-inspiring. Baseball fans had never seen anyone like him, and they flocked to the gate to see him hit.

[and] helped the fans of the nation, young and old, forget the past and the terrible fact that they had been sold out, that's all the **epitaph** I want," said Ruth.

Along Came Ruth

The arrival of Babe Ruth in New York City caused the turnstiles to spin like never before at the Polo Grounds, which the Yankees had shared with the New York Giants since 1913. Attracted by Ruth's fantastic long balls, fans flocked to ballparks to watch the Babe in action. In 1920, Ruth's first season in New York, the Yankees became the first major-league team to draw more than one million fans (1,289,422) in a single season.

As the owner of the Polo Grounds, the Giants were not happy playing second fiddle to the guests, and they declined to renew the Yankees' lease, forcing Ruth's team to search for a new home. In February 1921, the Yankees purchased ten acres of property from the estate of William Waldorf Astor at 161st Street and River Avenue in the west Bronx, directly across the Harlem River from the Polo Grounds.

The Yankees announced the construction of baseball's first triple-deck park. With room for nearly sixty thousand fans, it would also be the first structure to be called a stadium. The new Yankee Stadium would favor left-handed power hitters—and Ruth specifically—with a right-field foul pole only 295 feet from home plate, a short distance for a home run. Because it was widely recognized that Ruth's tremendous drawing power had made the new stadium possible, Fred Lieb of the *Evening Telegram* called the stadium "the House That Ruth Built," and the name stuck.

Yankee Stadium opened on April 18, 1923, with all the ceremony fitting the new king of baseball stadiums. According

Yankee Stadium: From Bolts to Nuts

When the New York Giants told the Yankees to leave the Polo Grounds, Colonel Jacob Ruppert, co-owner of the New York Yankees, had declared, "I want the greatest ballpark in the world." He got his wish.

The Osborn Engineering Company of Cleveland designed the park. It was the first stadium to have three decks, the first to ring its grandstand with the sixteen-foot-tall copper frieze that became its trademark, the first to house nearly sixty thousand seats, and the first to have a flagpole and commemorative plaques in the field of play.

The White Construction Company of New York broke ground on the site on May 5, 1922. Incredibly, the stadium was built in only 348 working days and at a price of $2.5 million. The steel framework eventually involved 2,200 tons of structural steel and more than one million brass screws. Materials used to form the playing field included 13,000 cubic yards of earth, topped by 116,000 square feet of sod.

The original Yankee Stadium opened in April 1923, with a crowd of more than seventy-four thousand in attendance. Ruth hit a homer to help beat the Boston Red Sox 4–1.

New York governor Al Smith is shown throwing out the ceremonial first ball before the first game at the original Yankee Stadium in 1923.

to *The New York Times*, 74,217 fans packed themselves inside, and thousands more were turned away by the fire department, "convinced that baseball parks are not nearly as large as they should be."

In pregame festivities, John Philip Sousa and the Seventh Regiment Band raised the **Stars and Stripes** and the Yankees' 1922 pennant at the flagpole in deep center field. New York's governor, Al Smith, threw out the first ball. Ruth had told a reporter, "I'd give a year of my life to hit a home run today."

Not surprisingly, he did. Ruth christened the new ballpark in the Bronx by slamming the first home run in Yankee Stadium history—a three-run shot off pitcher Howard Ehmke to help the Yankees capture a 4–1 victory over the Red Sox, Ruth's former team.

The Bronx Bombers

The Yankees' new home gave them one of their most famous nicknames: the Bronx Bombers. Led by manager Miller Huggins, they ended their first season in the new stadium by reaching the World Series for a third straight year. The Yankees had played in the World Series in 1921 and 1922, each time facing the rival New York Giants in an all–Polo Grounds World Series. The

Ruth is tagged out while trying to get back to first base during a rundown in the second game of the 1922 World Series against the Giants at the Polo Grounds in New York. The game was called after ten innings because of darkness and ended in a 3–3 tie.

1921 Series was the first time that all the Series games were played at one stadium. Ruth hit his first Yankee World Series homer that year, but the Giants won the Series that year and again the next.

The Bronx Bombers again faced John McGraw's Giants in the 1923 World Series, the first Subway Series. The subway, a form of public transportation in the city, was a convenient way to travel between the two ballparks. Ruth batted .368, walked 8 times, scored 8 runs, and walloped 3 home runs to help the team win the first of its twenty-six world championships. Now owner Jacob Ruppert had the greatest ballpark and the greatest team.

Ruth won his first (and only) Most Valuable Player award that season. He posted a career-high batting average of .393, led the league with 41 home runs, and drew a

This is a ticket to Game Two of the 1922 World Series between the New York Giants and the New York Yankees. That game ended in a tie because of darkness, but the Giants won each of the other four games in the Series.

Ruth had another big season in 1923 and led the Yankees to the World Series against the Giants for the third year in a row. This time, the Yankees won in 6 games. A game program from the Series is pictured here.

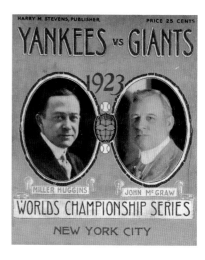

then-record 170 walks. He was the most feared batter in the game and would lead the league in walks 11 times, as more and more pitchers tried their best to avoid him.

After winning three straight American League pennants, the Yankees faltered and fell to second place in 1924, but the Babe had another marvelous season. He clocked 46 home runs, 19 more than the home run runner-up, and his .378 batting average was the best of anyone that season. However, there was also some sad news that year. A fire had destroyed three buildings at St. Mary's, including the administration building. Nobody was seriously harmed in the blaze, but virtually all of the school records were lost, including the files of a certain rough-and-tumble boy from Pigtown.

By the 1920s, Babe Ruth's popularity exceeded that of even the president of the United States. In this photo from 1923, he shakes hands with President Warren G. Harding before a game at Yankee Stadium.

A large sum of money was needed to rebuild the school, and Ruth came to the school's rescue by organizing a fund-raising effort. He arranged for the St. Mary's band to go along with the Yankees on a tour of American League cities and play concerts to raise money for reconstruction. Brother Matthias often accompanied the band, which pleased Ruth very much. The mischievous boy who went on to become the best player in the history of baseball never forgot about the students at St. Mary's. He often returned to the school to play catch with the boys and to encourage them to do their best.

Ruth poses with members of the St. Mary's band before a Yankee game in Philadelphia against the Athletics. Babe was helping his former school raise funds to rebuild after a fire.

CHAPTER 9

Guts and Glory

Sixty, count 'em, sixty. Let's see some[one] match that.

Throughout his early days with the Yankees, Babe Ruth was living at a fast, fun, and frantic pace. He bought Brother Matthias a new Cadillac and himself a red Packard roadster. He drove over the speed limit and was careless about following road signs, causing several accidents. On July 7, 1920, it was rumored that he had been killed when his car ran off the road and into a ditch in Pennsylvania. But Babe climbed out of that wreck. Over the years, he would survive many other mishaps behind the wheel. On June 8, 1921, he was arrested for racing well over the speed limit along a city street, fined $100, and sentenced to one day in jail. But the Yankees were playing that afternoon, so the police released him early and gave him an escort to the game, where he arrived just in time for the sixth inning.

Ruth, shown here behind the wheel of a car, loved automobiles. He was not a careful driver, though, and was involved in several accidents.

Another night, a policeman pulled Ruth over for driving up a one-way street and Babe joked that he was only going one way.

In the Public Eye

Babe Ruth was changing the way the game was played, making the home run the dominant aspect of the sport. His every move on the ball field drew attention, and so did his actions off the field. Babe and Helen adopted a baby girl named Dorothy in 1921. It was later alleged that Dorothy was Babe's daughter with another woman. His personal life was now covered in detail in the sports pages—and other sections of the papers as well. He was a full-fledged tabloid celebrity.

In this photo from 1922, Ruth plays with baby Dorothy at Fenway Park in Boston. The Yankees were in town to play the Red Sox, so Helen Ruth and the baby stopped by for a visit.

Ruth lived in an eight-room apartment suite in the elegant Ansonia Hotel, on the Upper West Side of Manhattan, home to many of the city's rich and famous. Due to the hordes of reporters and photographers stalking the building, Babe had to come and go through the janitor's entrance. Helen rarely came to New York, preferring to make a home with Dorothy at Home Plate Farm in Sudbury, Massachusetts.

Because of his larger-than-life personality, Ruth commanded more newspaper coverage in the 1920s than any other person in

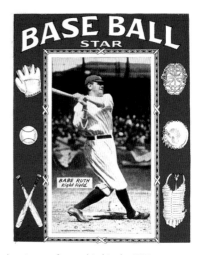

Ruth was featured in all sorts of publications and on items of every kind in the 1920s. He was pictured on the cover of this edition of *American Boy* magazine in 1925 and of this writing tablet.

the United States. Even people who weren't baseball fans knew his name. Babe Ruth was the most famous person in America. "I saw a man transformed from a human being into something pretty close to a god," said teammate Harry Hooper.

The Big Bellyache

Though very short and small (five feet six inches, 140 pounds), manager Miller Huggins was the big man in the Yankee clubhouse. A no-nonsense and feisty type, Huggins was known as Mighty Mite. He tried to keep Ruth in line by setting training rules regarding bedtime and diet. But Ruth's fondness for good times went beyond his loyalties to the team's training rules, and he often stayed out late drinking and overeating. His weight ballooned to more than 250 pounds.

Ruth fought frequently with his manager. Among Babe's many feuds with Huggins was one that developed over a 1925 "stomachache" that caused Ruth to miss the season's first 41 games and hit only .290 with 25 homers. On April 5, Ruth collapsed in a train station in Asheville, North Carolina, and was rushed to the hospital in an ambulance. Rumors of his death flew around the world. He was diagnosed with an ulcer that required an operation. (An ulcer causes bleeding into the stomach and can be very serious if not treated.) Most believed that his off-the-field eating and drinking habits had a lot to do with him becoming ill. Babe's six-week hospital stay was referred to as the Bellyache Heard 'Round the World.

Miller Huggins was the Yankees' manager from 1918 until his death in 1929. He was diminutive in size, but didn't back down from the bigger Ruth.

Ruth returned weak, having lost thirty pounds, and unable to swing the bat with his usual force. Pitchers were not afraid of him and hardly ever walked him anymore. Adding insult to injury, Huggins suspended Ruth for nine days for not following orders and fined him $5,000—ten percent of his salary—and called Ruth out of shape and a waste of talent. The two developed a strong mutual dislike. At a time when newspapers were virtually the only way people got their news, the feud was front-page headlines. The Yankees finished in seventh place in 1925, the only bad season they had during the Ruth era.

Career Crossroads

Ruth's lifestyle was at last affecting his play. This was one of only two seasons between 1918 and 1931 when he failed to lead the league in home runs. Worse, on August 9, for the last time in his record-setting career, he was taken out of a game for a **pinch hitter**.

For a long time, Ruth's off-the-field activities had been baseball's worst-kept secret. Fans knew of his behavior only as gossip, so Huggins's suspension and fine served as a public punishment and thus a stern warning to the Babe to shape up. That winter at a baseball writers' dinner, Jimmy Walker, mayor-elect of New York, said in a speech that Ruth's poor play and boorish behavior had let down the young fans of New York who idolized him.

For a long time, Ruth's off-the-field activities had been baseball's worst-kept secret.

Ruth was deeply upset. Some claim that he cried. The Yankees had won three pennants but had just one World Series title to show for it. He sincerely felt he had disappointed his fans. When Walker finished speaking, Ruth stood up. He apologized to the fans and promised to be good. "I want the fans to know that I've had my last drink," he said to great applause. "I mean it. I'm going to work hard. And then you just watch me break that home run record next year."

Babe Ruth's career was at a crossroads. He would be thirty-one years old in 1926, and many thought he was over the hill. True to his word, Ruth rededicated himself to the game he loved. In the winter of 1925, determined to recapture his former glory, Ruth worked out every day in a gym with a personal trainer, Artie McGovern, lifting weights and playing handball. He went on a diet, took steam baths, and got lots of

After he was ill for much for the 1925 season, Ruth vowed to take better care of himself. He began a rigorous training program and reported to camp in great shape in 1926.

sleep. The extra pounds slowly melted away and his muscles strengthened. Ruth showed up for spring training at a taut 212 pounds.

A Yankees Revival

The 1926 Yankees won the pennant by three games over the Cleveland Indians. Ruth was a major factor in that winning season. He belted 47 home runs with 150 **runs batted in (RBI)** and a .372 batting average. Though the Yankees lost the World Series in seven games to the St. Louis Cardinals, Babe's mark on the Series was memorable.

Prior to Game Four, Babe went to a hospital to visit Johnny Sylvester, an eleven-year-old boy who had survived a horse riding accident. Johnny's father, trying to cheer up his son, had

In this photo, Ruth watches one of his record 15 career home runs in World Series games. Three of those homers came in one game against the St. Louis Cardinals in 1926 to set another mark.

sent a letter to the Yankees asking for a baseball autographed by Ruth. Instead, Babe decided to go to the hospital in person. To make Johnny feel better, the Babe promised to hit a home run for him in the next game. That game was the first World Series game ever broadcast on national radio.

Ruth hit a home run, then another, and then a third, becoming the first man to hit 3 home runs in a single World Series game. The record-breaking third homer was also the first ball ever hit into the center-field bleachers at Sportsman's Park in St. Louis. When the ball finally came down, excited radio announcer Graham McNamee called, "What a home run! That is a mile and a half from here."

The Yankees won the American League pennant in 1926, 1927, 1928, and 1932. They swept (won 4 straight games in) the World Series in three of those seasons. If Ruth's revival signaled the continuation of the Yankees' dynasty, the arrival of

Lou Gehrig put them over the top. Gehrig became the Yankees' starting first baseman in 1925, and from then until 1932, he and Ruth were the two greatest hitters ever to play together. Ruth and Gehrig finished first and second, respectively, in the home run race each season from 1927 to 1931. They scared opposing pitchers in a way two batters had never done before.

Murderers' Row

The 1927 Yankees won 110 games (then a league record) and lost only 44. The Yankees' batting lineup was called Murderers' Row because of the way they terrorized opposing

Four Yankees from one of the most powerful big-league lineups ever assembled pose before a game in 1927. From left to right are Earle Combs, Bob Meusel, Lou Gehrig, and Babe Ruth.

Babe and Lou

Ruth and Gehrig were both left-handed hitters, but they were very different people. If Ruth was a roller-coaster ride, Gehrig was smooth and steady. He became known as the Iron Horse by playing in an incredible 2,130 games in a row. Gehrig combined dependability with one of the greatest bats in baseball history.

Gehrig always played in Ruth's shadow. He hit after Ruth in the batting order. His homers didn't fly quite as high or as far. Because he played second fiddle to Ruth, Gehrig's productive career is often overlooked. Lou knocked in more than 100 runs for 13 straight seasons. In 1927, when Ruth hit 60 homers, Gehrig won the league's Most Valuable Player award because Ruth, as a previous winner, was ineligible. When it was suggested that Gehrig try to be more colorful, he said: "I'm not a headline guy. I knew that as long as I was following Babe to the plate I could have stood on my head and no one would have noticed the difference. When the Babe was through swinging, whether he hit one or fanned [struck out], nobody paid any attention to the next hitter. They all were talking about what the Babe had done."

Ruth and teammate Lou Gehrig (left) were different personalities. While Gehrig was mild-mannered and quiet, Ruth was effusive and boisterous.

pitchers. The heart of the order—Ruth, Gehrig, left fielder Bob Meusel, and second baseman Tony Lazzeri—all drove in more than 100 runs each. The team batting average was .307.

Ruth, already the first batter to slug 30, 40, and 50 home runs in a season, became the first man ever to hit 60 home runs in a season. He also had a .356 batting average with 164 RBI, even though he was often walked intentionally. Ruth was challenged for the home run crown by teammate Lou Gehrig, but Ruth had a spectacular finishing kick, hitting 17 home runs in September. Gehrig finished the 1927 season with 47 home runs, more than anyone other than Ruth had ever hit. Together they out-homered every team in baseball except one.

Babe Ruth hit his record-breaking 60th home run off pitcher Tom Zachary of the Washington Senators at Yankee Stadium on September 30, on the next-to-last day of the 1927 season. The ball rocketed into the right-field bleachers, which had come to be known as Ruthville because so many of his home runs landed in this area. In the inning after hitting that home run, when he went to his position in right field, fans waved handkerchiefs and the Babe responded with military salutes. In the clubhouse after the game, Ruth boasted, "Sixty, count 'em, sixty. Let's see some[one] match that." Nobody took the invitation for thirty-four years.

The 1927 Yankees—considered by many to be the best team ever—averaged more than 6 runs per game and wound up winning the American League pennant by 19 games ahead of second-place Philadelphia. They beat the Pittsburgh Pirates in 4 straight games in the World Series. Legend has it that the Pirates were so intimidated watching the Yankees take batting practice before Game One of the World Series that playing the games was a mere formality.

Ruth's Record Falls

In 1961, Roger Maris of the Yankees hit 61 home runs to break the record of 60 that Ruth had set in 1927. But some said that Maris had an important advantage. The 1961 season had 162 games, but the 1927 season had only 154 games. For thirty years after 1961, the records were listed separately. But the twin listing was controversial, implying to some that Maris's record was somehow inferior. In 1991, baseball voted to remove the distinction, giving the record fully to Maris. Mark McGwire (St. Louis Cardinals) surpassed the record with 70 homers in 1998, and Barry Bonds (San Francisco Giants) now holds the mark with 73 in 2001.

Yankees outfielder Roger Maris hits his 61st home run of the 1961 season. Maris's blast broke Babe Ruth's thirty-four-year-old record of 60 homers in a season.

Ruth launches home runs during batting practice before a World Series game against the Pittsburgh Pirates in 1927. The overmatched Pirates never had a chance, losing the Series in 4 straight games.

The next year, the Yankees did the same against the St. Louis Cardinals. It was the second straight Series sweep for manager Miller Huggins's team. Gehrig blasted 4 home runs in the 1928 Series, but Ruth made history by whacking 3 in one game for the second time in his career.

"No one hit home runs the way Babe did," said Dizzy Dean, a Hall of Fame pitcher for the Cardinals. "They were something special, like homing pigeons. The ball would leave the bat, pause briefly, suddenly gain its bearings, then take off for the stands."

CHAPTER 10

A Living Legend

If it wasn't for baseball, I'd be in either the penitentiary [prison] or the cemetery.

Babe Ruth was back on top, the toast of the town. His drawing power at the gate made him the highest-paid entertainer of the day. The nation would soon be in the Great Depression, with millions of people out of work and hungry. But when Babe Ruth held out for more money, nobody criticized him.

Although he was not well educated, Ruth could be wise at contract time. When an offer for the 1923 season came in at $50,000, Ruth countered with $52,000 because "I've always wanted to make a grand a week." By the end of the decade, Ruth was earning more than Herbert Hoover, the president of the United States. "So what?" said the Babe. "I had a better year than he did."

Ruth was discovering that his talents could reap huge financial rewards. In addition to his baseball

Ruth was a smart man at contract time. In this photo, he signs an agreement with New York Yankees owner Jacob Ruppert.

Ruth poses with teammate Bob Meusel (left) and Christy Walsh in this photo from the late 1920s. Ruth hired Walsh as his agent. Today, almost all big-league players have agents, but it was not a standard practice in Ruth's day.

salary, he was also earning money by endorsing products and appearing in advertising for tobacco, sports equipment, and breakfast cereal. He hired an agent, Christy Walsh, to help manage his finances.

Babe made a lot of money, but he spent it freely. As always, the Babe was very generous, lending money to friends and then forgetting about it on purpose. A big tipper, he sometimes left a $100 bill for a waitress. He liked to gamble; when he won, he shared his winnings with teammates.

The Great Depression

The Great Depression was a decade-long period of worldwide economic crisis. In the United States, the Depression began when the stock market crashed in October 1929. As a result of this crash, many Americans, as well as banks, lost money that they had invested in stocks (shares or portions of businesses). In the years that followed, millions of people lost their jobs and their homes, and many went hungry. The economy eventually recovered, in large part due to reform programs that President Franklin D. Roosevelt enacted, known as The New Deal.

The Babe felt he owed the game a great debt. "If it wasn't for baseball," he liked to say, "I'd be in either the penitentiary [prison] or the cemetery."

High Hopes, Broken Dreams

Tragedy struck in January 1929 when Babe Ruth's wife, Helen, died in a house fire at the farm. They had been unofficially separated since 1925. Fortunately, seven-year-old daughter Dorothy survived. Only a few months later, on April 17, 1929, on what was to be the opening day of the baseball season, Ruth married again. His new wife, Claire Hodgson, was an actress whose husband had died. The opening game was rained out, but when it was finally played the next day, Babe hit a home run for his new wife and saluted her with a tip of his cap.

Babe and Claire had actually been together for several years. Shortly after their wedding, Babe adopted her daughter, Julia, and Claire adopted his daughter, Dorothy. They lived in an apartment on Riverside Drive in New York City. In the ensuing years, Claire helped to slow down somewhat her husband's fast-paced life.

In 1929, the Yankees failed to make the World Series for the first time in four years. Also in 1929, the Yankees put numerals on their uniforms to match the player's spot in the batting order. The Yankees and the Cleveland Indians were the first two major-league teams to do so for a full season. Ruth was given

Ruth is pictured with his second wife, Claire Hodgson, in 1929. The two were wed the day before the baseball season opened that year.

Lou Gehrig (right) welcomes Ruth at home plate after Babe homered on opening day of 1929. Ruth went on to hit 45 more home runs that season.

number 3 because he batted third in the lineup. Near the end of that season, there was more tragedy: Miller Huggins died suddenly at age fifty-one. When the team heard the announcement of their manager's death, Ruth cried. Babe was now thirty-four, and he was hoping to be named the Yankees' new manager. He asked Ed Barrow, who now worked for the Yankees, for the job but was rejected. Bob Shawkey, who was the winning pitcher in the first game at Yankee Stadium in 1923 and now a coach for the team, was chosen by Barrow instead.

Before the 1931 season, Shawkey was fired. Ruth's hopes rose again. But this time, Joe McCarthy, the former manager of the Chicago Cubs, got the job. Ruth resented McCarthy from the start and never tried to get along with him. It was nothing personal, simply a belief on Ruth's part that the manager's job should have been his. But the Yankees' top executive was Ed Barrow, who felt that Ruth had never managed himself well enough to indicate that he could manage a team of twenty-five players. Ruth was hurt. He said, "I don't think Ed realized that I had matured, was finally a grown man with family responsibilities and not the pipe-smoking playboy he had pulled the covers off in that hotel room in 1918."

King of the Sluggers

The Philadelphia Athletics dominated the American League from 1929 through 1931, but Babe was still king of the sluggers. Although the Yankees had slipped, Ruth led or tied for the league lead in home runs each year from 1929 to 1931. He hit home run number 500 on August 11, 1929, and number 600 two years later. Asked if he had any superstitions when he hit a home run, the Babe joked, "Just one. I make certain to touch all four bases." (Of course, if a player does not touch the bases, his run does not count.) In all, Babe led the American League in home runs 12 times, including six consecutive seasons, from 1926 through 1931, when he averaged more than 50 home runs a year.

Babe Ruth's home runs traveled higher and farther than anyone had ever thought possible. In fact, the Babe's ability to hit long home runs created a new word—Ruthian—to describe any larger-than-life event or feat. Some experts also think foul poles were invented for him. There used to be only foul lines on the dirt, but to help umpires follow the high arc of his Ruthian clouts, stadiums installed an extended pole up into the stands. A ball hit to the fair side of the pole—or one striking the pole itself—was a homer.

In 1932, the advancing years and pounds seemed to catch up with Babe Ruth. His knees were aching, and for the first time in seven years, he did not lead the league in home runs. But even an over-the-hill Babe Ruth at thirty-seven was good enough for a .341 batting average with 137 RBI. His 41 homers were second to the 58 hit by Jimmie Foxx, who became the first slugger to approach Ruth's single-season record. The Yankees recaptured the top spot, winning the pennant by 13 games ahead of the Athletics.

The Called Shot

After a three-year absence, the Yankees returned to the Series in 1932. It was Ruth's seventh World Series appearance in twelve years. He was at his best in these October showdowns, and his most famous home run of all came in this Series. It occurred on October 1 at Wrigley Field in Chicago. Ruth had already angered the Cubs when he took one look at the park's cozy dimensions and grinned. "I'd play for half my salary if I could hit in this dump all the time," he said.

The Yankees were playing the Chicago Cubs in Game Three of the World Series. Charlie Root was pitching for the Cubs and the score was tied 4–4. Ruth had already hit a 3-run homer in the first inning, much to the pleasure of New York governor and Democratic presidential nominee Franklin D. Roosevelt, who was at the game.

When Ruth approached the plate in the top half of the fifth inning, the 49,986 Wrigley Field fans, who had heckled him lustily all day, now yelled insults about his age and weight. Some fans started throwing vegetables at him, while others tossed lemons. According to folklore, players on the Cubs bench were also directing taunts at the Babe in the form of racial slurs.

What followed depends on whose version of the tale you believe. Root threw strike 1, which the fans cheered. Ruth supposedly held up one finger and, according to Cubs catcher Gabby Hartnett, said, "It only takes one to hit it." Root followed by throwing a pair of balls, and then another strike. The count stood at 2–2. Wrigley Field was ready to explode if Ruth struck out.

Ruth stepped out of the batter's box. Raising his right arm, the Babe made a gesture. Some thought he pointed. Did Ruth "call" his home run—did he really predict that he would hit it? No one knows for sure. He may have been pointing to the pitcher, or showing the crowd that he still had one more strike. Another possibility is that he might have been gesturing at the Cubs bench, which was filled with players who were teasing him. Or, as legend has it, was he pointing to beyond the outfield fence to indicate where he would hit Root's next pitch?

With the fans on the edge of their seats, the big-swinging lefty launched that next pitch straight over the center-field fence to that exact spot, a towering hit that measured 435 feet. It was the longest home run ever hit at Wrigley Field. It was also Ruth's 15th, and last, World Series home run. But did Babe really call his shot?

The Babe never said he did, and he never said he didn't. But it does not really matter whether he actually "called" that home run. Whatever the facts may be, it is absolutely certain that Ruth always had a flair for the dramatic, and it was heroic enough that in the face of abusive taunts from a large, hostile crowd, he came through in the clutch and delivered the punishing, crushing blow that defeated them. The battle over what truly happened in that one moment of time so long ago may never be settled. Still, Babe's "called shot" remains one of the most legendary moments in World Series history. The Yankees went on to sweep the Cubs, the third straight time they won a Series without losing a game.

This is a World Series game program from 1932. The Yankees swept the National League champion Chicago Cubs in 4 games that year.

Did He or Didn't He?

Did Babe Ruth really call his shot? No one can be sure. Here are some eyewitness accounts.

Lou Gehrig, who was in the on-deck circle and followed with another homer on the next pitch, said, "Did you see what that big monkey did? He said he'd hit a homer, and he did."

"Ruth did point," said Mark Koenig, the Cubs' shortstop and Ruth's former Yankee teammate. "He definitely raised his right arm. He indicated [where he'd already] hit a home run. But as far as pointing to center . . . no, he didn't."

Pitcher Charlie Root firmly denied that Ruth had pointed at the fence before he swung. Root said, "If he had made a gesture like that, Ruth would have ended up on his [backside]." In 1948, when asked to play himself and re-create the scene for the film biography *The Babe Ruth Story*, Root flatly refused.

The one man who could definitely answer the question was not saying. "Why don't you read the papers?" Ruth liked to say while flashing a sly smile whenever he was asked if he had called the home run. "It's all right there in the papers."

This illustration shows an artist's depiction of Ruth's famous "called shot" against the Chicago Cubs in the 1932 World Series.

CHAPTER 11

The End of an Era

I won't play for [the Yankees] again unless I can manage, too.

By 1933, Ruth's face was everywhere, including in newspapers and on magazine covers. He had already made his first movie, a full-length silent picture called *Headin' Home*, in which he starred as a small-town baseball player who rises to fame in the big leagues. A candy company named a candy bar for him, but there was already one called Baby Ruth, named for the daughter of former president Grover Cleveland, so Babe Ruth's Home Run Candy was discontinued after a lawsuit. Composers

Ruth endorsed all sorts of products at the height of his celebrity. Pictured here are just a couple of those endorsements, for Puffed Wheat and a clothing manufacturer.

Babe Ruth Pays No Tax On His Size
He Is A Giant in Physique, Still His Royal Clothes Cost Nothing Extra On That Account

A babe is a tiny human sprite that a woman can hold in her arms.

But the Statue of Liberty would have an armful trying to hold Babe Ruth.

This young colossus, weighs two hundred and twenty pounds, is six feet two inches tall and measures forty-four and one-half inches around the breast.

That means the use of an enormous quantity of fifty-two inch cloth to cover him up.

But we make no assessment against him on this account. Whatever the extra cost is, we absorb.

Maybe you also are an unusually large man—and you want *your* clothes to fit, in spite of that fact. But no matter. The Royal Tiger does not *punish* you therefor—if your waist and breast are under forty-five inches.

No wonder big men come to Royal service for their clothes needs.

wrote songs about him. Ruth's popularity was at its height, even as his baseball ability was fading.

Declining Years

Babe Ruth remained productive in 1933, but his dominance as a power hitter was slipping. He hit 34 home runs and struck out 90 times, the second highest total in the league that season. The strikeouts only added to his popularity. Fans loved watching Ruth swing, miss, and wind up in a pretzel-like position almost as much as they enjoyed seeing him connect. Most of his weight was in his belly. When he struck out, as he did 1,130 times in his career, his thick body wound his thin legs like a corkscrew.

Fans loved watching Ruth swing, miss, and wind up in a pretzel-like position almost as much as they enjoyed seeing him connect.

Despite more frequent strikeouts, dramatic home runs were still his style. Babe Ruth hit the first All-Star Game home run in 1933 in Chicago, bringing instant publicity to this new midsummer contest. On the last day of the 1933 season, Ruth pitched all nine innings for a complete-game victory in what was his final appearance as a pitcher. Though he hadn't been a regular pitcher during his years with the Yankees, Ruth was sometimes called upon to pitch a game for the team in his later years. He did this stunt five times—often at the end of a season when the pennant race had already been decided—and he won all 5 games.

The Yankees missed the World Series three years in a row from 1933 to 1935, but Ruth still had milestones to reach. He hit his 700th home run on July 13, 1934. When he hit it, only two other players had hit more than 300. Babe Ruth was synonymous with the home run. He was the first hitter to reach 200, 300,

Ruth crosses home plate after hitting a home run in the first All-Star Game ever in 1933. The blast came off National League starting pitcher Bill Hallahan of the St. Louis Cardinals.

400, 500, 600, and 700 career homers. (Hank Aaron and Barry Bonds have since also passed the 700 mark.) Ruth batted .288 and hit just 22 homers in 1934. He seldom played entire games, being removed for a defensive substitute in the late innings. His power was fading, and the Iron Horse was set to take center stage: Gehrig won the Triple Crown in 1934, leading the league in batting average (.363), home runs (49), and RBI (165). That year was also Ruth's last with the Yankees.

Back in Boston

After the 1934 season, Ruth and Gehrig, along with twelve other stars of the day, traveled to England, France, and the Far East to play in a series of exhibitions and promote the game. (It was for this trip that he obtained his birth certificate and learned

Going, Going, Gone!

To understand just how unique Ruth's home run production was during his greatest seasons, consider this: in 1920 and again in 1927, Ruth single-handedly hit more homers than any team in the American League other than the Yankees (54 in 1920, 60 in 1927).

Ruth's career home run output was also distinguished. Although Hank Aaron and Barry Bonds eventually broke Ruth's career home run record, Bonds needed nearly 1,500 more at bats, and Aaron needed nearly 3,000 more at bats. Ruth belted his 714 home runs in only 10,616 plate appearances. If Ruth had maintained his home run pace (one every 14.9 plate appearances) and come to the plate as many times as Aaron did, he would have hit 938 homers.

The Atlanta Braves' Hank Aaron watches the flight of career home run number 715 in a game against the Los Angeles Dodgers in 1974. Aaron surpassed Ruth's career mark of 714 homers, which had stood since his retirement in 1935.

Ruth's fame extended beyond U.S. borders all the way to the Far East. Cheering crowds mobbed him in Japan in this photo from 1935.

of his actual birth date.) Ruth was beloved in Japan, where baseball had long been popular, and he was welcomed like a conquering hero, his motorcade passing thousands of cheering Japanese people.

The tour was considered a great success for further increasing the popularity of baseball in Japan. Two years later, Japan started its own professional baseball league. The tour gave Ruth exalted status in Japan. A decade later, during World War II, American soldiers yelled, "To heck with the emperor!" at the Japanese. The Japanese soldiers yelled back, "To heck with Babe Ruth!"

This is a Japanese book about Babe Ruth. The American star was very popular in Japan, where he and other stars played a series of exhibitions following the major-league season of 1934.

子どもの伝記全集
ベーブ・ルース
赤坂 包夫著

Ruth was now an international celebrity. During the overseas tour, a reporter asked the thirty-nine-year-old superstar if he would be back with the Yankees in 1935. "I won't play for them again unless I can manage, too," said Ruth. He wanted to manage the Yankees, but no offer was forthcoming. He was, however, offered the managerial job with the Yankees' minor-league club, the Newark (N.J.) Bears, but he turned it down.

The Boston Braves, a mediocre National League team, badly wanted Ruth to join their team to boost attendance. They hinted that he might one day take over as manager. Ruth liked the idea of going back to Boston. He asked Yankees owner Jacob Ruppert for his release, and on February 26, 1935, it was granted. "It would not have been fair to stand in his way," said Ruppert. Babe and his wife and two daughters moved to Boston.

Ruth is pictured with the National League's Boston Braves in 1935. Forty years old that year, he played poorly, but he did have one last hurrah with a big 3-homer game.

The Last Hurrah

With Boston, Babe served as a vice president and an assistant manager as well as a player. Sadly, his two executive titles meant little. He would never manage the Braves or any other team. After spending twenty-two seasons in pro ball, Ruth felt disrespected. The game he saved didn't want him anymore.

Playing in one of his final games for the Boston Braves, the forty-year-old Ruth enjoyed a last hurrah on May 25, 1935, when he belted 3 home runs out of Forbes Field in Pittsburgh. The third one, the 714th and last of his career, a shot of more than five hundred feet off Pittsburgh pitcher Guy Bush, was the first to clear the roof of the right-field grandstand at the park.

Five days later, he called an end to his career. "I've played my last inning of baseball," he said. "I'm through."

What a career it was! When he retired, he had more than twice as many home runs as the second man on the list, even

Ruth is pictured with wife Claire in the stands in Brooklyn on opening day of the 1936 baseball season. It was the first year after he retired as a player.

GEORGE HERMAN (BABE) RUTH
BOSTON-NEW YORK,A.L.;BOSTON,N.L.
1914-1935
GREATEST DRAWING CARD IN HISTORY OF
BASEBALL, HOLDER OF MANY HOME RUN
AND OTHER BATTING RECORDS. GATHERED
714 HOME RUNS IN ADDITION TO FIFTEEN
IN WORLD SERIES.

Pictured above is Babe Ruth's induction plaque from the National Baseball Hall of Fame and Museum. He was a member of the charter class of 1936.

though his opportunities were limited by 2,062 walks. In 2,503 games played, he had 2,217 runs batted in and scored 2,174 runs. He was the owner of 56 major-league batting records.

The year following the Babe's retirement, he was one of five players elected in the first National Baseball Hall of Fame balloting, along with Honus Wagner, Christy Mathewson, Walter Johnson, and Ty Cobb. Ruth's plaque calls him simply the "greatest drawing card in [the] history of baseball." The plaque makes no mention of Ruth's career pitching mark of 94–46 (for a .671 winning percentage) or his 2.28 earned run average. In World Series competition, he had a record of 3 wins and no defeats, with a 0.87 ERA, allowing only 19 hits in 31 innings. Ruth was so talented that had he remained a pitcher for his entire career, he probably would have made it into the Hall of Fame for his skill on the mound.

CHAPTER 12

Heading for Home

The only real game in the world, I think, is baseball.

Frustrated by his inability to land a managing job, Babe Ruth accepted a coaching position with the Brooklyn Dodgers in 1938. He also regularly took batting practice with the team to entertain fans that wanted another glimpse at the great slugger. The Babe coached first base for the last three months of the season, hoping to be promoted to manager, but that didn't work out. He was there to help fill empty seats, not to inherit the

manager's job.

Ruth was never asked to manage in the major leagues. He turned down a few chances to manage in the minor leagues, but the call to manage in the major leagues never came. The

Ruth is shown coaching first base for the Brooklyn Dodgers in 1938. He hoped it would lead to a managerial job, but that dream was never fulfilled.

1938 season was his final season in baseball. "I wanted to stay in baseball more than I ever wanted anything in my life," said Ruth.

Farewell to a Friend

Although they started as great friends, the relationship between Lou Gehrig and Babe Ruth had cooled. Some believe that Ruth made a pass at Gehrig's wife. Others think that the Babe said something negative about Gehrig's beloved mother; apparently Mrs. Gehrig had made a comment about how Ruth's daughter dressed. And, according to several sources, the pleasant relationship between the two men boiled over while on the exhibition tour of the Far East after the 1934 season. On the boat there, Gehrig felt that Ruth was paying too much attention to Eleanor, Lou's wife. Gehrig made it clear that he never wanted to speak to Ruth again off the field. The two did not trade words for the next five years.

In 1939, Gehrig was diagnosed with amyotrophic lateral sclerosis, forever after known as Lou Gehrig's disease. It was incurable and fatal. Although he started the 1939 season, Gehrig seemed to lack power and appeared clumsy on the field. He removed himself from the lineup on May 2, ending his incredible consecutive-games-played streak. On July 4, 1939, Lou Gehrig Appreciation Day was held at Yankee Stadium, and Gehrig delivered his famed farewell address. In part of it, he said, "Fans, for the past two weeks you have been reading about the bad break I got. Yet today I consider myself the luckiest man on the face of the earth. . . . So I close in saying that I might have been given a bad break, but I've got an awful lot to live for."

When Gehrig finished speaking, Ruth threw his arms around the big first baseman and hugged him. It was perhaps the first

Ruth greets Lou Gehrig with a hug on the day that his former teammate is honored at Yankee Stadium in 1939. Gehrig, who was forced to retire that year because of a rare illness, died less than two years later from the disease.

time the two had communicated in years. It didn't end their feud entirely, but it did soften their relationship. Ruth's impulsive show of affection brought tears to many. The National Baseball Hall of Fame inducted Gehrig immediately. The great first baseman died in 1941 at the age of thirty-seven.

The War Effort

In 1941, the United States began fighting in World War II. Babe Ruth participated in exhibition games and other special events to raise money for war charities. In August

Photographers snap Ruth's picture as he warms up in Yankee Stadium in 1942. Ruth was there to bat against legendary pitcher Walter Johnson in a benefit for World War II charities.

1942, he appeared for a benefit at Yankee Stadium, where the forty-seven-year-old legend batted against Walter Johnson, 54, a Hall of Fame pitcher who had played with the Washington Senators. Ruth drove one of Johnson's pitches into the right-field stands, sending the crowd of more than sixty-nine thousand fans home happy.

Ruth spent $100,000 on war **bonds**, which were sold to help fund the war effort, and he served as a spokesman to encourage others to invest in them. He volunteered to work for the Red Cross, made visits to veterans' hospitals, and also played in golf tournaments and bowling exhibitions to raise money for the war effort. The Babe was like a famous ex-president, creating a stir whenever he appeared in public.

Final Years

During his retirement years, Ruth lived with Claire in his New York apartment and enjoyed his wealth and fame. Dorothy and Julia had both left home and gotten married. He made a comfortable living just being Babe Ruth. He played himself in the 1942 movie *The Pride of the Yankees*, based on Lou Gehrig's life. To look athletic for the part, Ruth lost forty-five pounds in two months. This made him so weak that he ended up in the hospital, but he did recover before filming began.

In 1946, Ruth was stricken with throat cancer. The disease, and several months of treatment, took a lot out of him. He lost nearly eighty pounds. In February 1947, he went to Florida to rest in the sunshine. The new baseball commissioner, A.B. "Happy" Chandler, declared that Sunday, April 27, would be Babe Ruth Day in the major leagues.

Ceremonies were held in all major-league parks, but Yankee Stadium was the site of the most significant celebration. Visibly suffering from a terminal case of throat cancer, the fifty-two-year-old Ruth bent to the microphone to

A makeup artist preps Ruth for his role in the 1942 motion picture *The Pride of the Yankees*. Ruth played himself in the movie about former teammate Lou Gehrig's life.

The retired slugging star approaches the microphone before speaking to the crowd at Babe Ruth Day in 1947. More than sixty thousand fans at Yankee Stadium were there to salute him.

address the crowd. He wore his familiar camel's-hair overcoat and camel's-hair cap. He was thin and pale. Speaking with a hoarse voice, Ruth thanked the sixty thousand people in the stadium and the fans across the land, and said, "The only real game in the world, I think, is baseball. You've got to let it grow up with you, and if you're successful and you try hard enough, you're bound to come out on top."

The Babe Bows Out

A crowd of more than forty-nine thousand fans turned out on June 13, 1948, to celebrate the twenty-fifth anniversary of the opening of the House That Ruth Built. In sentimental ceremonies, Ruth's famed uniform number 3 was permanently retired by the Yankees, meaning the number would never again be worn by another Yankee player. His uniform was formally presented to the National Baseball Hall of Fame and Museum in Cooperstown, New York, where it would be hung in a special Babe Ruth Room.

In the late stages of his cancer, Ruth was no longer the hulking, domineering figure he once was. In a touching scene, using a bat to support his fragile frame, Ruth walked slowly to the microphone and spoke in a soft, raspy voice. Babe Ruth knew he was dying. He told the fans how happy he was to have hit the first home run at the stadium, and he bid them farewell. It was the Babe's final appearance at Yankee Stadium, the house that he frequently filled.

This is Ruth's famous uniform number, from the National Baseball Hall of Fame and Museum. Babe wore the number because he was the third hitter in the Yankee lineup. The Yankees retired the number 3 in 1948 to honor the slugger's great career.

Babe is pictured in 1948 at his final appearance at Yankee Stadium. The team celebrated the twenty-fifth anniversary of the stadium that came to be known as the House That Ruth Built.

Two months later, on August 16, 1948, Ruth died of throat cancer at Memorial Hospital in New York City at age fifty-three. Pallbearers carried Babe Ruth's body into Yankee Stadium after his death.

An estimated one hundred thousand mourners filed past Ruth's casket as it lay in the lobby of Yankee Stadium. Little Leaguers came wearing their uniforms, and ballpark vendors sold hot dogs, one of the Babe's favorite snacks. Six thousand mourners packed St. Patrick's Cathedral in New York City for his funeral three days later as another seventy-five thousand gathered outside in the rain.

New Yorkers pack both sides of Fifth Avenue to watch Babe Ruth's funeral procession in 1948. Ruth was fifty-three years old when he died of throat cancer.

The Ruth Legacy

The Yankees dedicated a monument to Ruth on April 19, 1949, eight months after his death. The inscription is memorably brief for such an outsize man. Three lines of gold-faced letters read: "A Great Ball Player/A Great Man/A Great American." The 4,700-pound monument joined similar tributes to Lou Gehrig and Miller Huggins already located within the field of play at Yankee Stadium. Fans could see the large stone monuments, giving some youngsters the impression that the remains of the Yankee greats were buried under those tombstones. (Though outfielders would sometimes have to dodge the monuments that stood near the center-field wall, they remained a quirky part of Yankee Stadium for decades.)

In fact, Babe Ruth was buried in the Cemetery of the Gate of Heaven, in Hawthorne, New York. At his death, *The New York Times's* obituary called Babe Ruth "a figure unprecedented in American life. A born showman off the field and a marvelous performer on it, he had an amazing flair for doing the spectacular at the most dramatic moment."

In 1954, Babe's widow, Claire, learned of a baseball program for teenage players called the Little Bigger League. She met with the organization and gave permission for the program to change its name to the Babe Ruth League, saying, "Babe Ruth was a man who loved children and baseball; he could receive no greater tribute than to have a youth baseball program named after him." Today, more than one million players compete on Babe Ruth League teams.

More than one million teenagers in the United States compete on Babe Ruth League baseball teams. This photo is from tournament action between teams from Nampa, Idaho (in the red helmets), and southern Oregon in 2005.

This postage stamp with Babe Ruth's likeness on it is from 1983. It was issued on the fiftieth anniversary of Major League Baseball's first All-Star Game.

Years after his death, Babe Ruth still remains baseball's most memorable and dynamic figure. His name is included in American history textbooks, and his image has graced U.S. postage stamps.

More than seventy years have passed since Babe Ruth last hit a baseball in an official game, yet he is still considered the game's greatest player. The honor endures over generations. In 1969, a national vote of fans named Babe Ruth the greatest player ever. In 1998, *Sporting News* magazine ranked Ruth number one on a list of the game's all-time best players. In 1999, fans named Ruth to Major League Baseball's All-Century Team, and that same year the Associated Press selected Ruth as the Athlete of the Century.

Ruth was a man of mythic proportions. His birthplace in Baltimore was turned into a museum so that his many admirers—who never even saw him play—could get closer to his legend. For Ruth was bigger in size, in feats, and in his appetite for life than anything anyone had ever seen. He was the kind of man who once said, "I swing big, with everything I've got. I hit big or I miss big. I like to live as big as I can."

The Babe Ruth Museum

Babe Ruth's birthplace on the second floor of a three-story brick house at 216 Emory Street was the apartment of his mother's parents, Pius and Anna Schaumberger. They rented the apartment in a building that is located a long fly ball from the ballpark where the Baltimore Orioles play their home games.

In the late 1960s, two decades after his death, Ruth's birthplace was in disrepair. The building was to be demolished when Baltimore officials stepped in to save the house as a national shrine. The building was restored, and with the help of Ruth's family, it became a museum.

The historic house was opened to the public in 1974. Exhibits include:

• *The 500 Home Run Club*: this exhibit honors Ruth and the twenty-three other major-league players (through the 2008 season) that have reached the 500-home-run milestone.

• *Babe Batted Here*: this exhibit displays artifacts of Babe's ball-playing youth, including the St. Mary's jersey he wore and the catcher's mitt he used.

• *Playing the Babe*: Ruth's life story was the subject of many films and television shows. This exhibit features memorabilia from those productions.

• *The Historic House*: visitors to the museum can see the upstairs bedroom where Ruth was born, furnished just as it was in 1895.

Glossary

amateur—an athlete who does not play for pay.

ball—any pitch outside the strike zone at which a batter does not swing. Four balls allows the batter a walk to first base.

batting average—the number of hits divided by the number of at bats. A season average of .300 or better is considered the mark of a good hitter.

bigotry—a hatred and intolerance of certain groups of people that is often racially motivated.

bonds—a certificate issued by a government or company promising to pay back borrowed money, plus interest, by a certain date.

bunting—batting by tapping the ball lightly so that the ball falls in front of the infielders.

double—a hit that allows a batter to reach second base.

discrimination—unjust treatment of people based on, for example, race, religion, or gender.

earned run average (ERA)—a statistic that measures how many runs a pitcher allows to the opposing team during a typical game. A mark of 3.50 or lower is the sign of a solid pitcher.

epitaph—a statement commemorating a deceased person.

groundout—a play in which a batter gets out after hitting a groundball to an infielder.

home run—in baseball, a hit that allows a player to run around all four bases and score a run. Commonly called a homer.

major league—the highest level of professional baseball in the world. Currently there are two major leagues: the American League and the National League.

minor league—any professional league other than a major league.

pennant—the league championship in the American and National Leagues. The two pennant winners meet in the World Series. In Babe Ruth's day, the pennant went to the first-place team in each league. Today, each league has two rounds of playoffs, with the champion earning the pennant.

pinch hitter—a substitute for another teammate at bat.

racial slur—an insulting remark often related to the color of one's skin.

racists—people who believe that one race is superior to all others and judge others on the basis of their race.

runs batted in (RBI)—a statistic that counts when a player causes another player to score a run. A player can also get an RBI by hitting a home run. Gaining 100 or more RBI in a season is considered good.

shutouts—games in which the losing team does not score.

singles—hits that allow the batter to reach first base.

slugger—in baseball, a hard-hitting batter.

spring training—the period of practice and exhibition games in professional baseball that begins in late winter and goes until the start of the season in spring.

Stars and Stripes—the flag of the United States.

stealing—in baseball, when a runner on base runs to the next base as the pitcher starts to throw his pitch instead of waiting until the batter hits the ball.

stereotype—a conventional, oversimplified image of a person or a group.

truancy—the act of being absent without permission.

Uncle Sam—a slang term for the United States government.

walk—a free trip to first base for a batter after a pitcher has issued four balls during one at bat.

World Series—a best-of-seven-games series to determine the Major League Baseball champion. The winners of the American and National Leagues meet each fall in the World Series.

Bibliography

Books

Adomites, Paul, and Saul Wisnia. *Babe Ruth: His Life and Times.* Lincolnwood, IL: Publications International, Ltd., 1995.

Creamer, Robert W. *Babe: The Legend Comes to Life.* New York: Simon and Schuster, 1974.

Eisenberg, Lisa. *The Story of Babe Ruth: Baseball's Greatest Legend.* Famous Lives series. Milwaukee: Gareth Stevens Publishing, 1997.

Gershman, Michael. *Diamonds: The Evolution of the Ballpark.* Boston: Houghton Mifflin Company, 1993.

Macht, Norman L. *Babe Ruth.* Baseball Legends series. New York: Chelsea House Publishers, 1991.

Montville, Leigh. *The Big Bam: The Life and Times of Babe Ruth*. New York: Doubleday, 2006.

Pietrusza, David, Matthew Silverman, and Michael Gershman, eds. *Baseball: The Biographical Encyclopedia*. New York: Total Sports Illustrated, 2000.

Rothgerber, Harry and Brother Gilbert. *Young Babe Ruth: His Early Life and Baseball Career, from the Memoirs of a Xaverian Brother*. Jefferson, NC: McFarland & Company, 1999.

Ruth, George Herman. *Babe Ruth's Own Book of Baseball*. New York: G.P. Putnam's Sons, 1928.

———. *The Babe Ruth Story*. As told to Bob Considine. New York: Pocket Books, 1948.

Articles

Vaccaro, Mike. "The House That Ruth Built." *New York Post*, September 17, 2003.

New York Times. "74,200 See Yankees Open New Stadium, Ruth Hits Home Run." April 19, 1923.

New York Times. "Babe Ruth, Baseball's Great Star and Idol of Children, Had a Career Both Dramatic and Bizarre." August 17, 1948.

Web Sites

Babe Ruth Birthplace and Museum. www.baberuthmuseum.com

Babe Ruth League, Inc. http://www.baberuthleague.org/

Babe Ruth quotes. www.baseball-almanac.com/quotes/quoruth.shtml

National Baseball Hall of Fame and Museum. www.baseballhalloffame.org

Major League Baseball Statistics and History. www.baseball-reference.com

Official site for Babe Ruth. www.baberuth.com

Official site for Lou Gehrig. www.lougehrig.com

Official site of the New York Yankees. www.yankees.com

Source Notes

The following citations list the sources of quoted material in this book. The first and last few words of each quotation are cited and followed by their source. Complete information on referenced sources can be found in the Bibliography.

Abbreviations:

BRLT—*Babe Ruth: His Life and Times*
BLCL—*Babe: The Legend Comes to Life*
BR—*Babe Ruth*
BRS—*The Babe Ruth Story*
BGL—*The Story of Babe Ruth: Baseball's Greatest Legend*
BB—*The Big Bam: The Life and Times of Babe Ruth*
BRO—*Babe Ruth's Own Book of Baseball*
YBR—*Young Babe Ruth: His Early Life and Baseball Career, from the Memoirs of a Xaverian Brother*
BRL—Babe Ruth League Web Site
BRBG—"Babe Ruth, Baseball's Great Star and Idol of Children, Had a Career Both Dramatic and Bizarre"
BBE—*Baseball: The Biographical Encyclopedia*
YONS—"74,200 See Yankees Open New Stadium, Ruth Hits Home Run"
HTRB—"The House That Ruth Built"
BRQ—Babe Ruth quotes
LG—LouGehrig.com

INTRODUCTION: Babe Ruth: Larger-than-Life Hero
   PAGE 1 *"Where the Babe was, center stage was."*: BRLT, p. 174

CHAPTER 1: Saloonkeeper's Son
   PAGE 2 *"I was a bum when I was a kid."*: BLCL, p. 29
   PAGE 3 *"I hardly knew . . . my mother hated me."*: BRLT, p. 22
   PAGES 5–6 *"The truant officer . . . he always got out."*: BR, pp. 14–15
   PAGE 6 *"I was a bum when I was a kid,"*: BLCL, p. 29
   PAGE 6 *"I had a rotten . . . time to get my bearings."*: BR, p. 2
   PAGE 6 *"Not that I enjoyed . . . the normal thing to do."*: BR, p. 3
   PAGE 7 *"Looking back . . . very badly, I took it."*: BR, p. 2
   PAGE 9 *"I was listed . . . and I guess I was."*: BR, p. 2

CHAPTER 2: A Fresh Start
   PAGE 10 *"[Brother Matthias] taught . . . right and wrong."*: BR, pp. 3–5
   PAGE 12 *"I'm proud . . . who speaks ill of it."*: BGL, p. 26
   PAGE 13 *"It was at St. Mary's . . . between right and wrong."*: BR, pp. 3–5
   PAGE 13 *"He was calm . . . you were sure in trouble."*: YBR, p. 11
   PAGE 14 *"A great silence . . . Matthias was one of these."*: BR, p. 4
   PAGE 14 *"I guess I'm too ugly,"*: BRLT, p. 25
   PAGE 14 *"I guess I'm too ugly,"*: BRLT, p. 25
   PAGE 15 *"He was livelier . . . held his own, too."*: BB, p. 22
   PAGE 15 *"had facial characteristics . . . thing to have."*: BB, p. 21

CHAPTER 3: Finding Direction

PAGE 18 *"I never would have played . . . the course of my life."*: BR, p. 6

PAGE 19 *"It wasn't that . . . built me [up]."*: BR, p. 4

PAGE 21 *"If you know . . . do it yourself?"*: BRLT, p. 28

PAGE 21 *"As I took the position . . . Striking out batters was easy."*: BR, p. 7

PAGE 21 *"I never would have played . . . the course of my life,"*: BR, p. 6

PAGE 23 *"Roth the Speed Boy,"*: BLCL, p. 45

PAGE 23 *"the Bayonne Fence Buster."*: BLCL, p. 46

PAGE 27 *"speed boy,"*: BLCL, p. 45

PAGE 27 *"the most promising young ballplayer I've ever seen."*: BBE, p. 314

PAGE 27 *"I guess I must . . . 'I'll play. When do I start?'"*: BRO, p. 10

CHAPTER 4: Becoming the Babe

PAGE 28 *"There were moments . . . if I could make the grade."*: BR, p. 11

PAGE 28 *"There goes our ball club!"*: BLCL, p. 52

PAGE 28 *"He is going . . . Baseball Team."*: BLCL, p. 52

PAGE 29 *"You'll make it, George,"*: BR, p. 19

PAGE 30 *"I was 19 and . . . in the country,"*: BR, p. 10

PAGE 32 *"Anybody who eats . . . has got me,"*: BLCL, p. 221

PAGE 32 *"You want to go . . . not a circus act."*: BB, p. 37

PAGES 32–33 *"There were moments . . . to go back to St. Mary's."*: BR, p. 11

PAGE 33 *"he's one of Jack Dunn's babes."*: BRLT, p. 34

PAGE 34 *"Brother, this fellow . . . to a training camp."*: BB, p. 37

PAGE 34 *"My jaw must have . . . head with a bat."*: BR, p. 10

CHAPTER 5: From Baltimore to Boston

PAGE 36 *"Going to the Red Sox . . . the baseball walk."*: BRO, p. 14

PAGE 39 *"Going to the Red Sox . . . the baseball walk."*: BRO, p. 14

PAGE 41 *"He didn't drink . . . he'd ever been with a woman."*: BB, p. 44

PAGE 42 *"You're doing fine, George. I'm proud of you."*: BR, p. 42

CHAPTER 6: Pitching for a Living

PAGE 44 *"I didn't think . . . took my time in Boston."*: BRO, p. 15

PAGE 45 *"People sometimes . . . didn't like Babe Ruth."*: BLCL, p. 20

PAGE 46 *"That's all right, Ernie, I'm not particular."*: BR, p. 27

PAGE 48 *"I can remember . . . names don't stick,"*: BB, pp. 318–319

PAGE 49 *"I don't room . . . with his suitcase."*: BLCL, p. 222

PAGE 49 *"To understand him . . . He wasn't human."*: BLCL, p. 319

PAGE 50 *"In the Red Sox days . . . took my time in Boston."*: BRO, p. 15

PAGE 51 *"I ate my . . . get my chance."*: BRS, pp. 29-30

PAGE 53 *"I told you . . . National League bums."*: BLCL, p. 130

CHAPTER 7: The Changing World

PAGE 54 *"I'll win more . . . pitching every fourth day."*: BLCL, p. 187

PAGE 56 *"It wasn't a love pat. I really socked him."*: BR, p. 39

PAGE 57 *"The more I see . . . out of mythology."*: BRLT, p. 45

PAGE 58 *"I'll win more . . . pitching every fourth day,"*: BLCL, p. 187

CHAPTER 8: Babe's Big Move

PAGE 65 *"If my home run . . . epitaph I want."*: BR, p. 77

PAGES 69–70 *"If my home run . . . epitaph I want,"*: BR, p. 77

PAGE 70 *"the House That Ruth Built,"*: BB, p. 174

PAGE 71 *"I want the greatest ballpark in the world."*: HTBR, p. 5

PAGE 72 *"convinced that baseball . . . they should be."*: YONS

PAGE 72 *"I'd give a year of my life to hit a home run today."*: BB, p. 176

CHAPTER 9: Guts and Glory

PAGE 76 *"Sixty, count 'em, . . . match that."*: BLCL, p. 309

PAGE 78 *"I saw a man . . . to a god,"*: BB, pp. 14–15

PAGE 80 *"I want the fans . . . record next year."*: BLCL, p. 275

PAGE 82 *"What a home . . . from here."*: BRLT, p. 146

PAGE 83 *"I'm not a headline guy . . . what the Babe had done."*: LG

PAGE 85 *"Sixty, count 'em, . . . match that."*: BLCL, p. 309

PAGE 87 *"No one hit home runs . . . take off for the stands."*: BRQ

CHAPTER 10: A Living Legend

PAGE 88 *"If it wasn't for baseball . . . or the cemetery."*: BRQ

PAGE 88 *"I've always wanted to make a grand a week."*: BLCL, p. 24

PAGE 88 *"So what? I had a better year than he did."*: BLCL, p. 351

PAGE 89 *"If it wasn't for baseball . . . or the cemetery."*: BRQ

PAGE 91 *"I don't think Ed . . . in that hotel room in 1918."*: BR, p. 167

PAGE 92 *"Just one . . . touch all four bases."*: BRQ

PAGE 93 *"I'd play for half . . . in this dump all the time,"*: BLCL, p. 360

PAGE 93 *"It only takes one to hit it."*: BLCL, p. 361

PAGE 95 *"Did you see . . . he'd hit a homer, and he did."*: BRLT, p. 174

PAGE 95 *"Ruth did point . . . no, he didn't."*: BLCL, pp. 366–367

PAGE 95 *"If he had . . . on his [backside]."*: BLCL, pp. 366–367

PAGE 95 *"Why don't you read . . . there in the papers."*: BLCL, p. 368

CHAPTER 11: The End of an Era

PAGE 96 *"I won't play . . . unless I can manage, too."*: BRLT, p. 197

PAGE 100 *"To heck with the emperor!"*: BBE, p. 985

PAGE 100 *"To heck with Babe Ruth!"*: BLCL, p. 22

PAGE 101 *"I won't play . . . can manage, too,"*: BRLT, p. 197

PAGE 101 *"It would not have been fair to stand in his way,"*: BB, p. 338

PAGE 102 *"I've played my last inning . . . I'm through."*: BB, p. 340

CHAPTER 12: Heading for Home

PAGE 104 *"The only real . . . I think, is baseball."*: BLCL, p. 419

PAGE 105 *"I wanted to stay . . . anything in my life,"*: BB, p. 348

PAGE 105 *"Fans, for the past two weeks . . . an awful lot to live for."*: LG

PAGE 109 *"The only real game . . . come out on top."*: BLCL, p. 419

PAGE 113 *"a figure unprecedented . . . most dramatic moment."*: BRBG

PAGE 113 *"Babe Ruth was . . . named after him."*: BRL

PAGE 115 *"I swing big . . . as big as I can."*: BRQ

Image Credits

About the Author

David Fischer has written for *Sports Illustrated for Kids* and *The New York Times,* among other publications, and has authored or coauthored numerous books on sports, including *Greatest Sports Rivalries, A Yankee Stadium Scrapbook, Obsessed with Baseball,* and *Roberto Clemente: Trailblazer of the Modern World.* A lifelong Yankees fan, he currently lives in New Jersey and is a frequent visitor to Babe Ruth's shrine in Monument Park with his wife, Carolyn, and his children, Rachel and Jack.

Index

Aaron, Hank, 99
Alcohol, drinking, 6, 41, 49, 78, 79, 80
Amateur, 23, 116
Babe, origin of name, 33
Babe Ruth League, 113
Ball (called pitch), 56, 116
Baltimore Orioles. *See also* Dunn, Jack
  bike-riding antics, 32
  contract sold to Boston, 39
  contract with, 27, 28, 34
  debut with, 37–38
  down to minors and back, 41–42
  historical overview, 36–37
  majestic home run for, 33–34
  poor attendance and tough decision, 37–39
  raw rookie year, 32–33
  rookie challenges, 30–31
  spring training, 29–34
Barrow, Ed, 58–60, 91
Batting averages
  Babe Ruth, 50, 73–74, 81, 85, 92
  in Dead Ball Era, 47
  defined, 116
  Jack Dunn, 26
  Lou Gehrig, 98
Bigotry, 15, 116
Bike-riding antics, 32
Birth, of Ruth, 2, 44, 98–100
Black Sox scandal, 63, 68
Bonds, 107, 116
Boston Braves, 101–102
Boston Red Sox. *See also* World Series
  buying Ruth's contract, 39
  "Curse of the Bambino," 66
  rookie year, 39–41
  selling Ruth to Yankees, 65–66
  spring training, 44–45
  war-shortened season (1918), 60–61
Bunting, 47, 116
Career crossroads, 80–81
Carrigan, Bill, 41, 51, 52–53

Catchers, 20–21, 30, 39, 41, 55, 93
Childhood
  drinking alcohol, 6
  early Baltimore years, 3–9
  financial hardships, 4
  as Little George, 2
  mischievous acts, 6–7
  parents giving George up, 7–9
  skipping school, 5–6
"Curse of the Bambino," 66
Daughters, 77, 89, 90, 108
Dead Ball Era, 46, 47
Death/funeral, 111–112, 113
Death rumors, 76, 79
Discrimination, 16, 116
Donovan, "Wild Bill," 42, 45–46
Double, 42, 116
Dunn, Jack
  bike-riding antics and, 32
  biographical sketch, 26
  as legal guardian, 28
  offering professional contract, 27, 28
  Ruth impressing, 25–27
Earned run average (ERA), 49–50, 51, 103, 116
Egan, Ben, 30–31, 39
Endorsements, 89, 96
Epitaph, 70, 116
Federal League, 36–37, 64
Fighting and belligerence, 15–17, 56–57, 59–60, 78–79
Final years, 108–112
Frazee, Harry, 57–58, 60, 66
Gambling scandal, 63, 68
Gehrig, Lou, 83, 84, 85, 87, 90, 95, 98, 105–106, 108, 112
Gowdy, Hank, 55
Great Depression, 88, 89
Groundout, 52, 116
Hanlon, Ned, 26, 36–37
Home run(s)
  Aaron breaking record, 99
  all-time leaders, 68, 99
  called shot, 1, 93–95

career totals, 102–103
Dead Ball Era and, 46
declining years, 92, 97–98, 102
defined, 116
dominant aspect of game, 77
first of 714, 45
500 Home Run Club, 115
inside-the-park, 52
intentional walks and, 46, 85
justifying salary, 66
last one hit, 102
long, majestic, 33–34, 45, 57, 92
Maris breaking record, 86
Murderer's Row and, 83–87
new, improved baseball and, 67–68
photographs of Ruth and, 67, 69, 82, 87, 91, 98
pitching reducing career number of, 50, 60–61
predicting before hitting, 1
promising to hit, 15, 82
saving baseball, 68–70
on school team, 22
season-leading, 74, 83, 85, 91
single-season records, 62, 67, 85
stadium built for, 71–72
in World Series, 51, 52, 73, 82, 93–95
Hooper, Harry, 40, 41, 78
Huggins, Miller, 72, 78–79, 87, 90, 112
International tour, 98–101
Landis, Kenesaw Mountain, 63, 64, 68
Lazzeri, Tony, 85
Legacy, of Ruth, 1, 112–115
Lewis, Duffy, 40
Lifestyle. *See also* Fighting and belligerence
  affecting play, 80
  cars, driving and, 76–77
  eating/weight problems, 31–32, 78–79
  home with Helen, 53

Lifestyle (*cont.*)
late-night stunts, 58–60
moving on up, 42–43
rough edges, 46–48
self-discipline and, 56–57
women and parties, 49
Major league, 3. *See also*
Boston Red Sox; New York
Yankees; World Series
in Baltimore, 36–37
contracts sold, 27, 39
defined, 116
discrimination and, 16
Federal League, 36–37, 64
first full season, 49–50
rookie year, 39–41
Ruth records, 102–103
sent to minors from, 41–42
Manager, desire to be, 101,
104
Maris, Roger, 86
Marriages, 43, 90
Matthias, Brother
fan letter from, 42
guiding Ruth in baseball,
17, 18–19, 21, 22–23, 25,
28–29
new Cadillac for, 76
photograph, 13
running St. Mary's, 12–14
Ruth's love for, 13
temperament of, 13–14
touring with Yankees, 75
Meusel, Bob, 84, 85, 89
Military draft, 54
Minor league, 25–27, 36–39,
41–42, 116
Morrisette, Bill, 23, 34
Most Valuable Player award,
73–74
Movies, 96, 108
Murderer's Row, 83–87
Museum, Babe Ruth, 115
New York Yankees. *See also*
Home run(s); World Series
best team ever, 85
Bronx Bombers, 72–74
career crossroads, 80–81
last year with, 98
new stadium for, 70–72
revival, 81–84
Ruth sold to, 65–66
weight problems, 78–79

Nicknames, 15–17, 23, 33, 48
Pennant, 51, 66, 72, 74, 80,
81, 82, 85, 92, 116
Pigtown, Baltimore as, 5
Pinch hitter, 80, 116
Pitching
Dead Ball Era and, 47
less and less, 61–62
playing on off days, 57–59
punching umpire after, 56
Red Sox reputation, 50–51
at St. Mary's, 21, 22, 23–27
in World Series, 52–53
Providence Grays, 41–42
Public attention, 77–78, 96–
97, 98–101
Racial slurs, 15, 93, 116
Racists, 16, 116
Robinson, Jackie, 16
Runs batted in (RBI), 81, 117
Ruth, Claire Hodgson, 90–91,
102, 108, 113
Ruth, George "Big George,"
2, 3, 7–9, 43, 59. *See also*
Ruth's Café
Ruth, Helen Woodford, 41,
43, 49, 53, 77, 90
Ruth, Kate, 2, 3, 8, 14
Ruth's Café, 3–5, 6–8
Salaries, 34, 38, 39, 51, 66,
88–89
Saloon. *See* Ruth's Café
Shawkey, Bob, 45, 91
Shore, Ernie, 39, 46, 56, 57
Shutouts, 51, 117
Singles, 51, 117
Slugger, 1, 117
Speaker, Tris, 40
Spring training, 29–34, 44–
45, 58, 81, 117
Stars and Stripes, 72, 117
Stealing, 47, 117
Stereotype, 15, 117
St. Mary's baseball. *See also*
Matthias, Brother
about, 18
as alternative to fighting, 17
coming of age with, 19–21
George's prowess, 19–22
impressing Jack Dunn,
25–27
leaving for professional
career, 28–29

natural pitching talent, 21
playing amateur ball outside,
22–23
playing catcher, 20–21
star of, 22
St. Joe's showdown, 23–25
talent from day one, 18–19
St. Mary's Industrial School
about, 9, 10–12
bigotry, hateful names, and
fighting, 15–17
fund-raising effort for, 75
George staying for good,
14–15
going off to, 9
orphan myth and, 10
proud homecoming to,
34–35
reason for going to, 7–9
trades taught at, 11–12
Truancy, 5–6, 117
Umpire, punching, 56
Uncle Sam, 54, 117
Walk(s)
career total, 103
defined, 117
intentional, 45, 85
record number of, 74
ruining perfect game, 56–57
Walsh, Christy, 89
World Series
Black Sox scandal, 63, 68
calling home run in, 1,
93–95
defined, 117
lifetime statistics, 103
losing to Cincinnati (1919),
62–63
Red Sox and, 49–53, 60–
61, 66
winning and not playing in
(1915), 49–51
winning and starring in
(1916), 51–53
winning with scoreless
pitching (1918), 60–61
Yankees and, 72–74, 80,
81–82, 85–87, 90, 93–
95, 97
World War I, 54–56, 58–
59, 60
World War II, 106–108

Discover interesting personalities
in the Sterling Biographies® series:

Muhammad Ali: *King of the Ring*

Marian Anderson: *A Voice Uplifted*

Neil Armstrong: *One Giant Leap for Mankind*

Alexander Graham Bell: *Giving Voice to the World*

Cleopatra: *Egypt's Last and Greatest Queen*

Christopher Columbus: *The Voyage That Changed the World*

Jacques Cousteau: *A Life Under the Sea*

Davy Crockett: *Frontier Legend*

Marie Curie: *Mother of Modern Physics*

Frederick Douglass: *Rising Up from Slavery*

Amelia Earhart: *A Life in Flight*

Thomas Edison: *The Man Who Lit Up the World*

Albert Einstein: *The Miracle Mind*

Anne Frank: *Hidden Hope*

Benjamin Franklin: *Revolutionary Inventor*

Lou Gehrig: *Iron Horse of Baseball*

Matthew Henson: *The Quest for the North Pole*

Harry Houdini: *Death-Defying Showman*

Thomas Jefferson: *Architect of Freedom*

Joan of Arc: *Heavenly Warrior*

Helen Keller: *Courage in Darkness*

John F. Kennedy: *Voice of Hope*

Martin Luther King, Jr.: *A Dream of Hope*

Lewis & Clark: *Blazing a Trail West*

Abraham Lincoln: *From Pioneer to President*

Jesse Owens: *Gold Medal Hero*

Rosa Parks: *Courageous Citizen*

Jackie Robinson: *Champion for Equality*

Eleanor Roosevelt: *A Courageous Spirit*

Franklin Delano Roosevelt: *A National Hero*

Babe Ruth: *Legendary Slugger*

Jim Thorpe: *An Athlete for the Ages*

Harriet Tubman: *Leading the Way to Freedom*

George Washington: *An American Life*

The Wright Brothers: *First in Flight*

Malcolm X: *A Revolutionary Voice*

7-12